EARLY CHILDHOOD
Care and Education

EARLY CHILDHOOD
Care and Education

Editors

V.K. Rao

S. Khurshid-ul-Islam

Commonwealth Publishers

Early Childhood: Care amd Education
© 2017 Editor
ISBN-81-7169-472-1

Published by
COMMONWEALTH PUBLISHERS (P) LTD.
4831/24, Govind Lane,
Ansari Road, Darya Ganj,
New Delhi - 110002
Ph. : 23272541, 23242541
e-mail : commonwealthpublishers2016@gmail.com

Distributed by :
ARJUN PUBLISHING HOUSE
4831/24, Govind Lane,
Ansari Road, Darya Ganj,
New Delhi - 110002
Ph. : 23272541, 23242541
e-mail : arjunbooks2001@gmail.com

Laser Typesetting by :
Dimple Computers
Delhi

Printed at :
Roshan Digital Printers
Delhi

Preface

The nation's children are a supremely important asset. Their nurture and solicitude are our responsibility. Children's programme should find a prominent part in our national plans for the development of human resources, so that our children grow up to become robust citizens, physically fit, mentally alert and morally healthy, endowed with skills and motivations needed by society. Equal opportunities for development to all children during the period of growth should be our aim, for this would serve our larger purpose of reducing inequality and ensuring social justice.

The needs of children and our duties towards them have been expressed in the Constitution. The Resolution on a National Policy on education, which has been adopted, gives direction to State Policy on the educational needs of children. The state shall take steps to provide free and compulsory steps to provide free and compulsory educational for all children up to the age of 14 for which a time-bound programme will be drawn up consistent with the availability of resources. In organising services for children, efforts would be directed to strengthen family ties so that full potentialities of growth of children are realised within the normal family, neighbourhood and community environment. This book describes remedial techniques and methods for overcoming disorders in early childhood education.

Editor

Contents

1

Pre-School Education—Growth and Development

In the early part of the twentieth century most of the kindergarten schools were attached to the institutions established mostly by the missionaries. To them goes the credit of popularising the kindergartens in India. These institutions were not the typical kindergartens as envisaged by its founder. These kindergartens were later Indianised as Balwadis' or 'Shishuvihars' Sholapur kindergarten schools were started in 1901-1902 with the intention of training teachers. In 1907, Mrs. Annie Besant, who was British by birth, became the President of the International Theosophical Society after the death of its founder, Col. Olcott, who had started many schools for the young children in the city of Madras and its suburbs. According to Trilokekar, "Mrs. Annie Besant came to India because she felt that to serve India was her mission in life. India was the country she adopted her own." She stirred the Indians to free their country through her home rule movement. It was at this time that a number of schools for children and colleges for men and women, both in the North and South, were run by her on idealistic lines. She started a school at Adyar near Madras which was later shifted to Rishi Valley where the Theosophical Society had purchased property for educational work.

During 1920-30, most of the institutions concentrated their activities in the South India with a few beginnings in the North. In Eastern India, in 1918, Mrs Besant started the Central Hindu College at Banaras with the help of Dr. George Arundale who came to India at her call. In the Western India. Gijubhai Bhadeka started the first Montessori School in India in 1920. According to Ranjit Bhai. "The name of Gijubhai should be written in golden letters in the history of National Movement because he started his institution in 1920". In 1924 he opened his first training centre, Dakshinamurti Training College at Bhavanagar. This was followed by the formation of Nuton Balashikshan Sangh in 1926 covering both Gujarat and maharashtra.

This organisation was founded for the cause of child education. Two experimental schools, one in Gujarat and the other in maharashtra, were started by it for the children of pre-school age. Nutan Bal Shikshan Sangh also organized a training Centre at Dadar in 1938. In 1945, the sangh started its rural Centre of Pre-School Education at Bordi in District Thana. This centre was named as Gram Bal Shiksha Kendra. In 1935 and 1936 the nutan Bal Shikshan Sangh shifted its Headquarters to Bombay and set up a permanent training centre for the pre-school teachers.

In 1934, Dr. George Arundale had succeeded Mrs. Besant as the President of the Theosophical Society. The school started by her at madras had already been shifted to Adyar. Mrs. Besant had expressed a desire that there should be an educational institution in the vicinity of Theosophical Society. It was to abide by her wish that Dr. Arundale and mrs. Rukamani Devi started the Besant Memorial School at Adyar in 1934 with a Montessori section attached to it. This was known as Adyar Montessori Centre. The contribution of AMC is no less important. It idealised Montessori education even in rural areas of the country. Dr. Arundale, however, felt that no educational work would be complete without a training centre for the teacher. Education of children depends on the right type of teacher. He, therefore, invited Dr. maria Montessori to India in 1939 and started Montessori Training Centre for teachers. Dr. Montessori readily accepted the invitation of Dr. Arundale and conducted the first training course with Montessori methods There was a great response from the people when she went to different parts of the country to conduct various training courses. She conducted special teacher training courses at Madras, Kodaikanal, Ahmedabad, Bombay and Karachi. In the meanwhile second World War, started. Dr. Montessori was not permitted to leave India which she resented. But she utilised her time fruitfully to strengthen the Montessori movement in India. Montessori was invited to India again in 1947 to start Arundale Montessori Training Centre for teachers at Adyar in the extensive gardens named after Col. Olcot. But partition of the country at the time of independence, prevented many teachers from the North in joining the course. The then government of Travancore financed the training and also deputed teachers for this course.

The Indian movement in the field of pre-school education owes much to Annie Besant and Tagore in the early part of the 20th century. There were a few private enterprises in South India, who looked to "New Educational Movement" of Europe for a social change through education but the actual movement in India on a national scale was started by Annie Besant and Tagore. At that period, there were three types of institutions in the field of pre-school education India: (a) Institutions run by Theosophists; (b) Special type of schools for children of rich families run by Maharajas: (c) Schools and Centres in Gujarat and maharashtra, run by private individuals."

Other developments which took place in the pre-school movement in India were opening of Shishu Vihar Mandal at Yeotmal in Maharashtra and Centre of Cosmic Education at Allahabad in 1951, Happy Education Society at Delhi, Nai Taim Sangh at Wardha, Balniketan Sang at Indore in 1941 and the Association Montessori International in India. In 1944 the Central Advisory Board of Education (CABE) gave concrete suggestions for the reorganisation of pre-school education in India. John Sargent, in his book, Education, Society and Progess, points out:

> "....An adequate provision of pre-primary instruction should be regarded as an essential adjunct of any national system of education... In urban areas, where sufficient children are available within a reasonable radius, separate nursery schools or classes should be provided, but elsewhere, nursery classes should be attached to junior basic schools. Pre primary education should in al cases be free. Nursery schools and classes should invariably be staffed with women teachers specially trained for this purpose."

The CABE Report recommended that we should make a provision of 1,000,000 free places in many schools or classes for children in the age range 3 to 6 years. The Sargent Report suggested "free attractive pre-school education by the State.. in order to pay attention to a very impressionable, plastic and educationally potentially potent period of child's life.

Pre-Basic education plan

In 1937, Mahatma Gandhi did not have any plan for the child below seven years. But when he returned from jail in 1944 he had realised that he could not neglect the child below 7, then he gave his views on the pre-basic education of children under 7, which was termed as pre-basic education. This education, according to Gandhiji, should be conducted in cooperation with parents and community. The first pre-basic education school, established under Kasturba Memorial Trust, started functioning in July 1945 at Sevagram, under the guidance of Smt. Shanta Narulkar. Owing to more urgent calls on the national resources since 1947, it was not possible to plan any comprehensive development for the education of children of pre-school age until 1951, when Indian Council for Child Education was formed with Smt. Sarladevi Sarabhai as its President. The Ministry of Education, Government of India, in their report Progress of Education in India 1947-52, remarked:

> "Pre-primary education was for the most part confined to urban areas and has been the responsibility of parents... The policy of the govt in this respect has been that of assistance and encouragement. There has been a sudden expansion of this education in the middle of the quinquennium due partly to Madam Montessori's stay in India: but mainly due to organised efforts and ability of certain private bodies."

Pre-School education during five-year plans

In the First Five Year Plan, though the need for pre-school education was stressed but no definite financial provision was made for this purpose. In this regard. All India Education Conference on the problems of Child Education held at Indore in 1955 remarked.

"It is also surprising that neither the First Five Year Plan nor Community Development Projects mention anything about the need for pre-primary education nor do they make any provision for the purpose. Obviously the importance of this subject has escaped the attention of the planners." As a part of the first Five Year Plan the Central Government set up a Central Social Welfare board with the object especially of assisting voluntary agencies in organising welfare programmes for women and children. The CSWB assisted 2128 institution of which 691 were child welfare institutions. But in the first five year plan, out of 169 crores provided for the development of education, no allocation was made for the pre-school education.

In the later part of the Second Pan the Planning Commission made a provision for child welfare and education. This was done on the recommendation of the Child Care Committee which was appointed by the Central Social Welfare Board. Out of Rs. 307 crores provided for education during the second plan no special provision was made for the pre-school stage. Assuming 3 to 6 as the normal age range for nursery schools or classes, there were over 40 million children in this age group in 1960-61. The growth of pre-school institutions and enrolment in these institutions is reported by Sargent.

"Since independence the number of institutions

has grown from 303 in 1951 to 1909 in 1961 and is expected to reach 35000 by 1966. The enrolment has risen from 22,000 in 1951 to 1,21,000 in 1961. In addition there are a good many children below the age of 6 in ordinary primary schools. ...In the same ten years the number of teachers has gone up from 866 to just over 400, of whom 3600 are women. The percentage of those who are trained has remained steady around 65."

It was only during the Third Five year plan that the Government formally recognised the need for pre-school education. The Planning commission had asked the Central Social Welfare Board to appoint an expert committee to survey and report on child care in the country. For the first time, pre-school education was recognised by the Government of India as the base of national system of education, and thus a national policy was to be formulated for the cause of pre-school education. The report of the expert committee, set up by the CSWB, is a land mark in the history of pre-school education as for the first time its recommendation to the government covered the "total child", including education, health, nutrition and recreation. The committee pointed out that pre-schools should be self-sufficient and should be started by the voluntary agencies. Balwadis should be started both for rural and urban areas. These should be run by the Community development departments and Central Social Welfare Boards. As a result of these efforts the total number of Pre-school Child Care Centres was estimated to be 3,500, which an enrolment of about 14.5 lakhs which was 35 percent of the total population of children between 3-5 years. This, according to Ranjit Bhai, was "a very bright account of people's response in the interest of child education". In 1961 there were about 5000 Balwadis with an enrolment of about 3,00,000 children. Of three about 2,500 were assisted by the Central and State Social Welfare boards. by the end of Third Plan the number of balwadis organised by these Boards rose to 5761. The Third Plan provided for the setting up of six training centres for Bal Sevikas. In the programmes for education Rs. 3 crores were allotted for child welfare and allied schemes at the Centre and about Rs. 1 crore in the States in addition to resources available under the community development and social welfare programmes. Schemes that were formulated by the Ministry of Education included improvement of the existing Balwadis, opening of new Balwadis, expansion of training programmes for Bal Sevikas and a number of other projects in which education, health and welfare services were integrated. Regarding the enrolment of children in pre-schools and Balwadis upto the end of Third Plan, Iredale points out. "The All India picture is more difficult to colour in any detail partly because of diversity of the agencies running both the schools and the teacher training programmes. Between 1951 and 1966 the known enrolment in mainly urban pre-primary schools in the country rose from 28,000 to 250,00, while in 1966 the number of children enrolled in Balwadis was claimed to be 600,000."

According to Arunt Thakkar "During the Third Plan, the grants-in-aid programme of the Central Social welfare Board gave an impetus to the promotion of pre-school education and 2174 pre-schools, Nursery schools, Montessori, schools kinder grated schools, pre-basic schools, and Balwadis." 4815 Balwadis were aided by the CSWB. Some Developments During 1966-1969 Period: In 1964, the Indian Association of Pre-school Education was formed. In 1966 the Education

Commission gave its suggestions for strengthening the pre-school education. The IAPE brought out a comprehensive document which dealt with such important problems as: Pre-school education for the rural and tribal children: education at the training centre; the system of pre-school education; recent trends in pre-school education; voluntary efforts in pre-school education; and pre-school teacher educations. In 1969 the national council of Educational Research and Training decided to set up the Department of Ore-primary and Primary Education. This department collaborated with other agencies and prepared courses of studies for the schools and also for the training of teachers.

It was suggested in the draft of the Fourth Five Year Plan that "in the field of pre-school education, government effort will be confined mainly to certain strategic areas such as training of teachers, evolving suitable teaching techniques, production of teaching materials and teachers' guides. In the Social Welfare sector, however, there will be a small provision for the opening of Balwadis, both in rural and urban areas". Children below 6 constitute nearly 17% of the total population of India and 15 million are being added every year. In the last two years of the Fourth Plan, services for 1 million additional children belonging to weaker sections were to be launched. In addition to this training of personnel through new types of training programmes were to be launched. Therefore, Fourth Plan period was marked by these developments in pre-school education. For example, a national seminar on the pre-school child, organised at Madras jointly by the international Children's Centre, Paris, and Indian council for Child Welfare, discussed three broad aspects of early childhood education, namely, health and nutrition objectives, educational and social objectives. in 1970, the sixth meeting of the IAPE was held. During this year, the pre-primary teacher education curriculum was developed by the NCERT. In 1971 the NCERT set up the Department of Pre-primary and Primary Education at its National Institute of Education and special attention was paid to teacher preparation. More literature was produced for the pre-school level. Seventh meeting of the IAPE in 1972, published its report on 'Relating Pre- school to Primary School. A national seminar on An Integrated Approach to the Pre-school Child' was also organised at Bangalore in 972. During this year the NCERT also published its report on 'Pre-primary institutions -Their Supervision'. The concept of supervision at the pre-school state has been discussed in this report. The evaluation instruments and directions for their use in making assessment of a pre-school were also included in this report. By the end of fourth plan the number of children benefiting from the various schemes had also increased significantly as pointed out by "By 1974 the number of children benefiting from nutrition schemes at feeding centres and Balwadis all over the country amounted to nearly 7 million, of which approximately 18,00,000 were in tribal areas and 17,00,000 in urban areas."

The draft report on Fifth year Plan recognised the importance of preschool education. The facilities of pre-schools were however, limited as is pointed out in the report:

> "The facilities available at present, are, however, limited to a number of privately run schools in urban areas and few thousands

> Balwadis and Anganwadis run under government auspice in social welfare sector. While it may be difficult to provide pre-school education facilities of any sophistication, the situation demands that some effort of an elementary kind be made immediately. It is, therefore, envisaged in the Fifth Plan that children's Play Centres for the age group 3-6 may be attached to selected primary schools. In addition to these centres, private agencies will be further assist in the strategic areas of teacher training, preparation of teacher guides and promotion of research for evolving methods of pre-school education suited to our condition."

The Fifth plan had the rural, tribal and slum areas as its target for child welfare. The Plan aimed at providing integrated services-health, welfare, education, nutrition and family planning -as bases to promote child welfare. During this Plan, 13 million children in the age group of 0 to 6 years were to be covered by extending integrated services to 18% of the total children in the weakest section of Indian Society. In the Fifth Plan Rs. 25 crores were provided for the educational component and Rs. 75 crore for the social welfare plan. A national Policy Resolution for children was issued in 1974.

As a result of this a National Children's Board was constituted. The Integrated Child Development Scheme was introduced in 33 experimental areas which provided supplementary nutrition, immunization, health check, referral services, nutrition, health education and Non-Formal education to children in the age group 0 to 6 years. Further, 117 ICDE experimental projects were introduced during 1978-80. The focal point of the ICDS projects provided services through Anganwadis which were run by a local voluntary worker who was assisted by a helper. The work of Anganwadi workers was to be supervised by a Mukhya Sevika.

For the first time the 'early childhood education' has been used in place of 'pre-school education' as the former is intended to be more broad-based and cover the entire period of crucial development upto 5 years. Special attention is to be paid to the children of under-privileged groups. The Sixth plan report says.

> "This early childhood stage is the period of maximum learning and intellectual developments of the child and hence of great potential educational significance. The present preschool child care programmes are limited to the distribution of food supplements and routine health cover; these contribute very little to the personality development of the child, especially to its intellectual, social and emotional growth. The concept of learning and development through play and joyful activities should be articulated, across age group, through an all round programme which should be comprehensive in scope, integrated nature and reinforced over long time. Organisation of a creche for children in the 0-3 age group and/or a Balwadi for 3-6 age group, with provision for educational toys, play equipment, learning materials and books for children's reading would be appropriate for this purpose."

The Sixth Plan provides an outlay of Rs. 2524 crore for

development of education and culture. Out of this Rs. 905.37 crores, 35.87% of the total outlay, have been allotted for the early childhood education which is highest amount ever allotted for this purpose. Following arc the agencies which manage the pre-school education in India:

Government agencies

Though education has been a state subject, yet the policies regarding pre-school education have been mostly framed and implemented by the Central level agencies like Central Social Welfare Board. Iredale observers. "The interesting and crucial point about pre-school education in India is that it lies mainly within the scope not of the Ministry of Education but of the ventral Social Welfare Board, whose brief is to develop pre-primary education in the country as part of family and child welfare schemes... At the State level too, most pre-primary education is handled by the Department of Social Welfare and is entirely unrelated to the work of Education department, through this pattern runs counter to the recommendation of Education Commission of 1966, in which close liaison between Education and Social Welfare as proposed together with a pre-primary centre within State institutes of Education." In most of the States the Director of Social Welfare controls the pre-schools through Bai Sevikas and Mukhya Sevikas.

Of late there are some more development. There is perhaps some Justification in entrusting the responsibility of pre-school education to the Social welfare departments. Pre-school education. Is viewed as a part of child and family welfare schemes. But for the education component of the pre-school programmes, especially in the mater of teacher preparation, the State Institute of Education are laying prominent role. For example, SIEs of Maharashtra, Rajasthan, Madhya pradesh and of other states have started working in the field of pre-school education. In Maharashtra a course has been drawn up combining the training for teachers for pre-primary and primary schools. In Rajasthan, Balwadis are functioning under the guidance of SIE. In Madhya Pradesh, the SIE has developed teacher training course on the pattern suggested by the National Council for Teacher Education.

Private bodies

The private sector in India has played a significant role for the spread of pre-school education. They stepped up their activities after the visit of Madam Montessori to India. Many Montessori and Nursery schools as well as training centres were started. According to Ranjit Bhai; 'Voluntary efforts in the field of pre-schools education made it possible to popularise nursery and Montessori schools, which were hitherto considered centres for children of rich families only.... Even to day the field of education is managed by private individuals or societies and the best schools or training institutions in India are run by private societies."

Semi-official and autonomous organisations

There are several national and international level organisations working in the fields of pre-school education. The names of national level organisations are given below:

1. Central social welfare board
2. Indian Council for Child Welfare
3. Indian Red Cross

4. Kasturaba Memorial Trust
5. All India Women's Conference
6. Montessori International Association in India. G. Nutan Balshikshan Sangh, Bombay
7. All India Cosmic Education Society
8. Kishore Dal, Patna
9. Children's Education Society, Mysore
10. Happy Education Society, Delhi
11. City montessori Schools, Lucknow
12. All India Balkan-Ki-Bari
13. Indian Association for Pre-school Education
14. University colleges/Departments of Home Science
15. State Institutes of Education
16. National council of Educational research and training, New Delhi.

(a) *Central social welfare board:* The CSWB organises activities of pre-school through its State Departments of Social Welfare. These activities are organised as part of the family an child welfare schemes and are organised under three heads: health, nutrition, education and social welfare services. The State Departments/Boards of Social Welfare organise 'Balwadis'. The 'Balwadis' are day-care-centres' and 'only a losse approximation to the work 'Pre-school. In the towns there are nursery schools, whereas in the villages rural Balwadis are run. The CSWB gets funds from the Central Government on the recommendation of the Planning Commission. It also appoints nations committees to examine various issues pertaining to the child education and welfare schemes. Some time ago the CSWB appointed an expert committee to survey and report on child care in the country. The report of the committee was a most significant contribution because it asked the CSWB to cover the total child' including his health, nutrition, education and recreational needs. The CSWB also organises Bai Sevika Training Centres. (b) Indian Council for child Welfare: The ICCW organises programmes of child welfare. It also helps in running the Balwadis and Bai Sevika Training Centres. It collaborates with the International Children's Centre, Paris and the United nations Children's Fund in organising programmes of educational, social and nutritional nature. (c) Role of the NCERT: The National Council of Educational Research and Training has been actively associated with the Development of pre-school education in India. The Department of Pre-primary and Primary Education was set up in 1969. The department collaborated with other state and national level agencies and prepared courses of studies for the pre-schools and training of school teachers. The two teacher training courses prepared by the NCERT in collaboration with the National Council for Teacher Education are B.Ed courses.

The NCERT has also undertaken research projects for the developmental norms of Indian children in the age group 2 1/2 to 5. The Department of pre-primary an Primary Education was re-oraganised by the NCERT in 1975 and a separate Child Study Unit has since been set up. The CSU has brought out many useful publications on pre-school education and has also set up Children's Media Laboratory. The objective of setting up this laboratory is to develop inexpensive, non-formal effective media of educational and entertainment value for children in the age group of 4 to 8. Other activities of the CSU include organisation, of inservice courses for the pre-school teachers, undertake research in child development and several other activities at the national level. (d) Indian Association of Pre-School Education: The IAPE was formed in 1964. Since then it has been actively engaged in promoting the cause of pre-school education. It has brought out several publications. In addition to this, the IAPE teachers gives suggestions and recommendations on the various aspects of pre-school education. (e) Numerous other Organisations: All India Women's Conference, Guild of Service, Madras, Indian Red Cross, Bharat Sewak Samaj, All India Balkan-Ki-Bari, Bal Niketan Sang, Kishore Dal, Nutan Bal Sikshan sangh, Bombay, Children's Education Societies in Gujarat Karnataka, Delhi and Association Montessori International in India which organises Montessori schools, teachers training programmes, day-care-nurseries, pre-primary schools, Balwadis and child health centres. (f) Education and Community development Departments in various States run Nursery Schools, Nursery Teachers' Training colleges and Pre-Basic Schools. (g) Labour Welfare and Health Departments in States organise Creches, Maternity Centres, Day Care Centres and Health Centres. (h) Public Sector undertakings have set up pre-schools in different cities under their own educational authorities. (i) The various religious bodies have started pre-school along with the primary, secondary and higher secondary schools., (j) The CARE operates its nutritional programmes in collaboration with different States. (k) The University Department of Child Development and home Science colleges also have training programmes, mostly for women, at the early childhood education level. (I) Some national level Institutes like B.M. Institute of Child Development. Ahmedbad and Child Study Unit at the Tata institute of Social Sciences Bombay are also working for the cause of pre-school education.

Children are not passive recipients of media content; they select and use the media according to the motives, predispositions, and cognitive capacities brought from previous experience. Nevertheless, exposure can affect both what they learn and the way they behave, even thought these effects may depend on individual characteristics of the child. Children learn a great deal from the media even though entertainment rather than instruction is usually their principal goal in using media. Usually the more attention the child devotes to tne media stimulus, the greater the learning. Children are typically more attentive to characters who have high status or power or who are similar to themselves in sex, age, or ethnic background.

A number of factors determine which components will be learned most easily from a film or other stimulus when a variety of behaviours is presented. The components most readily learned are those that are obvious and easily observed, those that are at least partially familiar to the child, and those to which he can easily give verbal labels. In some instances, behaviour for which the model is rewarded or punished is also recalled better than behaviour followed by no consequences. All of these factors operate in relation to the child's level of cognitive development. Researchers of differing theoretical persuasions generally agree that preschool children are less likely than older children to produce verbal spontaneously or to use them in an abstract way in learning situations. In the case of observational learning, one result of this "production deficit" seems to be that preschoolers retain less than older children from a given observational experience. In one study, four-year-old children were able to reproduce about half as many actions from a simple film as the seven-year-old when each group watched it without instructions. When an adult verbally labeled the actions and the child repeated the labels, four-year-olds remembered as much as the older children. The additional labeling did not improve the amount retained by the seven-year-olds, presumably because they had spontaneously labeled the actions themselves. These findings suggest that, under natural conditions, preschool children may retain less from any single media exposure than elementary school children. It is of interest to note in this context that many cartoons feature an announcer who maintains a loud running verbal description of the action. Preschool children are also likely to rely on their immediate perceptual experience even when they have some conceptual knowledge that conflicts with it. For example, in a study testing conservation of liquids, children were shown two identical beakers of water, then the water from one was poured into a beaker of a different shape. Preschool children were more likely to recognise that the amount of water was the same when the second beaker was screened from view than when they were looking at it. They apparently had some conceptual understanding that the amount was the same, but the knowledge was overwhelmed by the fact that the beaker looked different. This feature of the child's cognitive development might lead him to believe and accept what is presented in the media even when it is contradicted by verbal or conceptual knowledge. Difficulty in making fantasy-reality distinctions is a related characteristic of young children's cognitive functioning.

The absence of these distinctions is dramatically illustrated by the disinterest shown when a presidential assassin is shot on television or a man walks on the moon. Differentiation of fantasy and reality is particularly difficult to learn from television because it is such a realistic medium and because it presents both real and fictional events in similar ways. In sum, preschool children probably are more likely than older children to "believe" the immediate perceptual stimulus from the visual media and to have difficulty distinguishing real from unreal. They may retain less than older children from any one media exposure, but the repetition that occurs in the mass media probably eventually enables them to learn and retain much of the pervasive content. Elementary school children are more able to use verbal and conceptual knowledge to place in perspective what they see, but they often draw faulty conclusions from information they receive and do not consider mall possibilities. Therefore, they may still be more susceptible than adults to persuasive messages and other forms of media influence. Once a child has learned and retained something new from the media, that information is available for him to use in his own behaviour. Thus, presentation of new responses is one means by which the media can affect behaviour even though children do not perform all the new actions they learn through observation. In other instances, the media do not teach anything new but affect the likelihood that the child will perform actions he already knows. Bandura proposes two categories of such effects: inhibition or disinhibition and social facilitation. In the case of behaviour that is socially disapproved or likely to be punished, observation may either reduce or increase the child's inhibitions. Behaviour that is not likely to be forbidden may also be facilitated by observation. When a child hears a story about a toy train and then decides to play with his toy train, the story has apparently been the stimulus for a behaviour that is neither new nor forbidden.

The only other medium reaching large numbers of preschool children is books. During the elementary school period, children are exposed to comic books, movies, radio, newspaper comic strips, and magazines as well. Television, comic books, movies and comic strips are generally categorised as pictorial media, all appearing to serve similar functions. Children who are high users of one are likely to be high users of the others, but not high users of printed media. When television is first introduced to a locale, the time spent on other pictorial media declines, but time devoted to printed media remains unchanged.

Use of all media increases until about age twelve, after which the time devoted to pictorial media declines. Boys and girls use all media about equally except comic books, which are used more by boys. Children from lower-class homes use pictorial media more than middle-class children, and black children have more exposure to them than whites even with social class controlled. Evaluation of mass-media effects is based primarily on two types of studies. One type is essentially correlational; some feature of media exposure or preference is related to some aspect of children's behaviour. Such studies provide information about naturally occurring media use, but do not permit inferences about the direction of effects. Although social scientists investigated and criticised violence in movies, radio, and comics during the 1930s and 1940s, the advent of television brought violence and crime to American children in much larger quantities and with a more realistic and compelling means of presentation than had been the case with other media. in a recent federally sponsored report on mass media and violence, the available literature was reviewed and the authors concluded that media violence stimulates aggressive behaviour under a variety of circumstances, particularly in the young. At the same time, they recommended more research. As a result, twenty-three studies of television and social behaviour are nearing completion at this writing.

Violence and morality in current media

A content analysis of the prime-time and Saturday morning programs on the major television networks was conducted in 1967 and 1968. Programs were analysed in three categories: comedy; crime, western, action-adventure; and cartoons. News and documentaries were excluded. Violence was defined as "the overt expression of force intended to hurt or kill". Approximately 80 percent of all programs contained some violence. About two-thirds of the "comedy" programs contained violence with an average of 4.5 incident per program. Virtually all programs in the crime-western-action-adventure category and over 90 percent of the cartoons contained violence. The frequency of violent acts in the crime-adventure category was 8.7 per hour; in the cartoons it was 22.5 per hour.

Aggression and illegal actions are often portrayed as successful and morally justified despite the fact that the majority of adult Americans disapprove of the amount and kind of violence shown on television. Law enforcement officers and other heroes use violence as frequently as villains and often break laws and moral codes as well. In both adults' and children's programs, these socially disapproved methods of attaining goals are more often successful than socially approved methods. While criminal and illegal activities frequently escape punishment, goodness alone is rarely sufficient to achieve success. Even as the positive consequences of violence are implicitly emphasised, the distasteful bloody, or painful results are excluded in a great majority of programs. The fundamental philosophy manifest in most current television programming is that the end justifies the means and the successful mean's are often immoral, illegal, or violent.

A slightly different picture emerges from analyses of comic books and comic strips. In 1954, the Comic Magazine Association of America developed a code for voluntary regulation, apparently in response to organised public pressure. The code prohibits knife play, killing with guns, mugging, garroting, and strangling. Overt sexuality and the more horrible ghouls, werewolves and monsters are excluded. Although not all violence and crime were eliminated, this code was sufficiently that one of the major citizen's pressure groups deemed its semiannual monitoring of comic book content unnecessary by 1958. No more recent analyses have been located by this author, but one author suggests that comic books have returned to some of the pre-1954 vividness. The comic strip section in the newspaper is the one most often read by young children. Preference for television programs containing crime and violence is associated with aggressive and delinquent behaviour in boys during the elementary and adolescent years.

As people watch their preferred programs most often, it is reasonable to infer that aggressive and delinquent boys are exposed to more of the crime-violence program type than are other children. In one study, third-grade boys and girls were rated by their school classmates on scales of aggression. Their favourite television programs were classified into violence and non-violent categories. For boys only, the amount of violence in favored television programs was positively correlated with peer ratings of aggression. In this study as in other, overall exposure to television was not positively related to aggression.

Critics of the media agree that those who are predisposed to overaggressive and violent behaviour may be most likely to seek criminal and violent content, but assert that such content would be more difficult to find without the large daily doses available in the media. Furthermore, they hypothesise that observing media crime and violence produces disinhibition of these types of behaviour, regardless of the initial reason for exposure. They predict increased aggression and immorality as a result of exposure.

The empirical evidence for preschool and early elementary school-age children unequivocally supports the disinhibition hypothesis. Observation of aggressive behaviour produces increased aggression whether the model is live, on film, in commercial cartoons, or in a story.

Displays of rule-breaking and lack of self-control

also reduce children's moral inhibitions. In one study, a duty-pleasure conflict was established for elementary school boys by assigning each the responsible but boring job of watching a control panel that allegedly signaled flaws in a film being edited.

The film was shown just outside their range of vision, so that they had to leave the editing machine unattended in order to see it. Children who had previously seen an adult yield to the temptation of looking at the movie were more likely to do so themselves than were those who saw the adult remain at his job or who saw no model. Another aspect of mature self-control is the willingness to defer gratification in order to achieve more important rewards in the future. The ability to delay gratification is acquired gradually and with some difficulty by young children. Yet in television drama, immediate solutions to problems are emphasised. Most media presentations must create and resolve a plot in a brief time period. It is likely, therefore, that the media do little to help children develop the ability to defer gratification and may in some instances retard this development. One experimental study found that elementary school children who initially expressed a preference for delayed gratification were significantly swayed by observation of a model preferring immediate gratification. The change in outlook was maintained on retest a month later. A finding that high school students who were "high" television users were less likely than "low" users to endorse deferred gratification many partially reflect this media influence. Theoretically, observational learning could also promote acquisition of self-control and inhibition of socially disapproved action. However, it is most difficult to increase inhibition through presentation of models who resist temptation or engage in non aggressive activity.

In most studies, children who observed such model showed no more self-control and no less aggression than no-model control groups. Exceptions have occurred in a few experimental situations discussed in detail by Hoffman. Many children are exposed to media vice and violence every day without imitating these characteristics. Why do some children imitate and others not? One reason may be that some children receive training from parents and other socialising agents that provides them with alternative sets of values and methods for coping with frustration. Faced with a moral dilemma or interpersonal conflict, they have a variety of possible responses. Children without such alternative training are likely to rely heavily on the limited solutions learned from the media. For them, the media fill a void or, in violent families, replicate their home experience.

The notion that it is the children without strong countersocialisation who are most affected by media violence is partially supported by a recent study of elementary school boys. For boys who perceived that their parents clearly disapproved of violence, exposure to aggressive television programs did not affect attitudes toward aggression. Among middle-class boys whose parents communicated ambiguous values about violence, however, those who watched many violent programs approved of aggression and expressed willingness to use it more often than did boys with low exposure to such programs. Lower-class boys' attitudes were not related to television viewing regardless of parental values.

Once aggression is aroused in children by the media, many typical parent reactions are likely to perpetuate it. Both permissiveness and physical punishment usually increase rather than decrease aggression.

As both of these socialisation techniques are commonly used, it is likely that many children who are repeatedly stimulated to aggressive behaviour by the media start a chain reaction of parental responses that lead have a more aggression by the child. Thus, even if the media alone have a short-lived impact, they may serve as catalysts for more enduring effects. If a child perceives himself or his situation as similar to the person or situation in a film, he is more likely to imitate what he sees. For example, Boy Scout troops were shown a film of a boy their own age engaging in various activities. One group was told the boy was a Boy Scout with interests similar to their own, another group was told that he had very different concerns. Imitation was greater in the "similar model" condition than in the "dissimilar model" condition. Similarity of physical cues in the child's environment to those in the media also makes imitation more likely, so the sale of toys costumes, and other accouterments to accompany "Batman," "Superman," and similar programs probably stimulates considerable emulation of these figures. Cartoons are often thought to have less impact on children's behaviour than television programs portraying real people because they are less similar to real life settings. However, adults are not very good judges of the way children perceive programs. A young child may perceive himself as more similar to cartoon figures such as "Underdog", who shares his physical smallness, or "Bambi," who is concerned about maternal loss, than he does to an adult sheriff in a western.

Comparisons of cartoons with films containing real people suggest that cartoons are equally effective in stimulating unitative behaviour. Without contrary evidence, it should not be assumed that the Saturday morning violence parade has weak effects because it is in cartoon form. Effects on moral values and attitudes. Current theory and research on the development of moral judgment suggest that young children's moral standards and attitudes should be particularly affected by the fact the media violence and immoral behaviour are so often successful in goal attainment. Two important theorists, paget and Kohlberg, propose that young children are moral abdutists who judge right and wrong by the consequences of actions rather than by the intentions of the actor or by abstract moral principles.

Rewards and punishments not only regulate external behaviour, they define the morality of an action. The message of the media for young children, then, is likely to be that you can get away with violence and illegal activity, and that these actions are morally right. There is evidence that values and attitudes of children are affected in just this manner. Zajonc presented a radio "space" story portraying one pilot who was threatening and coercive toward his crew and one pilot who was friendly and understanding. In one version, the coercive leader succeeded; in the other, the affiliation-oriented leader succeeded. Preadolescent boys overwhelmingly endorsed the techniques of whichever character succeeded. In another study; boys who were high users of pictorial media scored higher than low users on a scale of "Children's Fascism" that included a variety of authoritarian and antihumanistic attitudes such a approval of the use of violence in solving interpersonal problems, endorsement of the acts of theft, murder, and sadism under certain circumstances, and acceptance of war in an unrealistic and glamorised form.

Another group of heavy-media users focused on the technical aspects of crime in describing a comic-book plot while low-media users focused more on the moral aspects. The positive rewards for aggression and amorality in the media have been stressed thus far, but there are also portrayals of punishment for crime and other moral transgressions. These might be expected to enhance children's moral behaviour by teaching them that "crime does not pay." Indeed, in experimental situations, children who see morally deviant or aggressive models receive punishment are less likely to imitate than those observing reward or no consequence for the same behaviour. That is, when a child observes deviant behaviour, punishment to the model reduces the likelihood that he will imitate. With a few exceptions, however, the groups which have seen a model punished behave similarly to groups exposed to no model. This comparison suggests that observing negative consequences does not make any positive contribution to moral behaviour; the child's actions are no more moral and no less aggressive than they would have been without any exposure to a deviant model.

Observing deviant behaviour, even when the model is punished, does have an effect that is absent when no model is presented; children learn and remember information about his actions.

This distinction between learning behavioural

imitation was demonstrated in a study of preschool children. Those who observed an aggressive model who was punished showed less behavioural imitation than children who have seen the same model receive reward or suffer no consequences, but they remembered just as much of his action as the other groups. Similarly, when children see a detailed bank robbery in a movie, they are likely to learn something about robbing banks even though the criminal is caught and punished in the end. Because the bloody and painful aftermath of violence is excluded from most television programs and comic books, some critics argue that the full power of observed negative consequences is not operating in the media. They apparently believe that violence, if portrayed should be presented realistically. In this author's opinion, such recommendations, could backfire and should not be implemented without considerably more research. Displays of painful reactions to aggression lead in some cases to increases in aggression rather than decreases. Juvenile delinquents were shown two films of a fight between two boys. One version centered on the aggressive actions of the winner, the other on the pain reaction of the loser. When subjects were angered, they displayed more interpersonal aggression after the pain-cues film than after the aggressive-action film. The presence of pain reactions in real-life aggression may also be an immediate cue that helps children to recognise the differences between media violence and real life. Finally, daily observation of blood and gore could result in desensitisation so that children's empathic reaction to pain would be blunted. Some writers believe that children are already desensitised to the violence that is currently depicted. The most effective policy the media could adopt is to reduce the number of presentations that teach and disinhibit antisocial behaviour. Portrayal of nonviolent and morally conforming characters may have some beneficial effects, but their influences is probably far outweighed by the effects of aggressive and deviant characters.

Emphasising negative consequences to aggressive and morally deviant characters is preferable to allowing such characters to go unpunished, but observed negative consequences do not usually lead children to develop more self-control or to act with less aggression than they would without such a media experiences.

Effects of media

Media presentations involving violence, danger, conflict, and tragedy do stimulate immediate emotional reactions. Siegel found that children watching an aggressive cartoon exhibited more signs of anxiety than those watching a nonaggressive cartoon. British children reported feeling upset by seeing killings on the "tele" and both humans and animals in several studies responded emotionally to seeing another of their species in distress. Children apparently react to media more intensely than adults. More important, they often interpret a plot differently and, as a result, respond emotionally to different aspects of its content. In an early study of movies, elementary school children frequently perceived the plot inaccurately, tended to focus on separate items in the film, and were less likely than older children to assimilate the content of the story. The differing interpretations by young children may lead them to react strongly to some stimuli that appear innocuous adults and vice versa. dia exposure, it appears that frequent and repeated exposure usually leads to gradual reduction of emotional responsiveness rather than to cumulative increases.

A process of adaptation or desensitisation seems to occur for most individuals. This process was demonstrated experimentally in a study of adults. Those who had previously seen an anxiety-arousing film showed less anxiety in response to a second film than those who had initially seen a neutral film or no film. While such adaptation may take longer for young children, they apparently undergo a similar process. The media could be used constructively to reduce irrational childhood fears.

In two studies, observing live or filmed models reduced phobic fears in preschool children. During a series of sessions children fearing dogs watched as another child or children played with a dog in a series of interactions that gradually became more fear-provoking. Fear reduction was measured in a behavioural rest; the final step in the rest required the child to remain in a playpen with a dog. The fearless models led to reduced fright both immediately after the treatment and on retest one month later. The most successful film presented multiple models-several children played with several dogs. From this exposure, a "sleeper effect" occurred, children were significantly less fearful on the retest after one month than they were on the immediate posttest. "Misterogers' Neighborhood" is one current television program specifically designed to reduce childhood fears. Through a combination of reassurance, demonstration, and fantasy, Misterogers attempts to counteract children's concerns that they will kill someone with their thoughts, be flushed down the toilet, be eaten by monsters, and so on. As the media can produce desensitisation and fear reduction in other situations, this program may well produce the intended effects, but direct evidence is lacking. For many children, television is the major source of information about the world outside their own homes and neighborhoods. It teaches them human personality types, sex and occupational roles, and about ethnic groups and social classes other than their own. What do mass media teach children about their social world?

As these characterisations probably fit readily into children's moral absolutism, the media be reinforcing a childhood tendency to stereotyped views of human personality rather than helping the child grow beyond this level.

In one survey, boys who were high users of pictorial media were more prone to social stereotyping than low users even when IQ, social class, and other relevant variables were controlled. Stereotyped sex roles-aggressive males and passive, domestic females-are overrepresented on television in comparison to the real world. Males are central characters much more often than females. When females are featured, they are less likely than the average American woman to have an occupation outside the home, especially if they are married or are mothers. In the traditional realms of marriage and family life, themes of fatalism and passivity are frequent, perhaps because women characters are not as readily permitted the favorite and most successful problem solution—violence.

Children have little direct contact with the occupational world, so they derive their knowledge about many occupations from the mass media. On television, professional and managerial occupations are overrepresented relative to the real world while skilled and unskilled labor are underrepresented. Positive attributes such as physical attractiveness, social skill, and intelligence are concentrated in high prestige occupations.

Questioning of elementary school children revealed that television was the major source of their knowledge about the nature and status of occupations such as lawyer and newspaper reporter, which are frequently shown on television but with which children have little personal contact. One might expect that frequent portrayals of high-status occupations would encourage children to set high personal aspirations, but available evidence contradicts this hypothesis. In one study, boys with high media exposure were less likely than low exposure boys to aspire to an occupation with higher status than their fathers. Instead, high media users were more likely to aspire to romanticised occupations such as those of FBI agent for boys and actress for girls.

Television perpetuates common occupational stereotypes such as burly truck drivers and cold, efficient nurses. Young children's ready acceptance of media stereotypes was demonstrated by exposing second-graders to a radio series about taxi drivers. One group heard supposedly fictional programs in which taxi drivers were aggressive, the other heard the same stories with nonaggressive endings. Children exposed to aggressive endings were more likely than those hearing nonaggressive endings to believe that the taxi drivers in the children's own small Pennsylvania town would behave aggressively.

Traditionally, minority groups have been excluded or presented in stereotyped form in the mass media. Afro-Americans usually have been servants and low-status workers, often with the shuffle and "Yes, boss" of Jack Benny's Rochester Marked changes have occurred in the last ten years.

Regular television series in 1968, according to one survey, presented Afro-Americans in positions of generally high status such as detective, physician, and nurse. Because black elementary school children report identifying with black television characters, these changes may well enhance the self-images of black children. Nevertheless, older programs are constantly rerun during the "children's hours" on television, so children are still exposed to overtly biased portrayals of black people. Unfortunately, there is no evidence for comparable changes in the negative pictures of other ethnic minorities or of the working class. What should the media teach children about the social world? Should they delineate the actualities or the ideals of this world? And whose ideals should be represented? Television and other media should present a wider diversity of life as it is and as it might be. Most television drama has a dreary predictability that excludes vast segments of real experience and possible life patterns.

Diversity in interpersonal style, family patterns, occupational activities, conflict resolution, and the life, could provide media users with many alternatives to help guide their own behaviour. Presentation of shadings between good and bad and of people honestly holding different beliefs and values could also facilitate the development of more mature modes of moral understanding among young children.

Television is a potential source of general information and language training as well as of social knowledge.

In one survey, first-grades in a town receiving television broadcasts had more advanced vocabularies than those in a town without television. Otherwise, most researchers have concluded from earlier studies that the many hours in front of the "tube" have little impact on children's cognitive functioning. "Sesame Street" is the most notable effort to use public television for teaching cognitive skills to young children. In its first year the program was designed to reach children from three to five, especially residents of disadvantaged urban areas.

The commercial techniques of fast action, animation, and slapstick humor were used quite successfully to attract and hold the interest of young children. In a sample of 943 children studied by the Educational Testing Service, nearly 90 percent watched the program at least occasionally. Half of the sample watched it four or more times a week. These figures do not represent the amount of viewing by children in general, however, because the majority of the sample was initially "encouraged" to view the program. The disadvantaged children who were not encouraged were probably more representative of others in that population; about half of them watched the program more than once a week. Evaluation consisted of pre- and posttests of the skills outlined in the goals of the producers; symbolic representation, problem-solving and reasoning. Children who often viewed the program showed greater gains than infrequent viewers. The evaluation was deliberately designed to reveal specific skills taught by the program rather than changes in general intelligence, partially because of the doubtful validity of standard intelligence tests for disadvantaged children. Although the frequent viewers showed the most gain on the tests administered, they were also more skilled than infrequent viewers before they saw "Sesame Street." Analysis before and after the program of two subgroups matched for age demonstrated that the gains by high viewers were a result of watching the program, not just a function of their initial ability or motivation. Many questions about the impact of "Sesame Street" remain to be answered and more research will undoubtedly be forthcoming. There is little information now, for instance, about the duration of its effects, the extent to which initial school performance is benefited, the effects on skills other than those tested, or the comparative merit of other methods of teaching.

Proposal interpersonal behaviour such as cooperation, helping, understanding another's feelings, coping calmly with frustration, and following rules are frequent themes in the "Misterogers' Neighborhood" program. The effects of that program on children's interpersonal behaviour in the nursery school are currently under study by this author and her colleagues, but final results are not available at this writing. Positive effects of exposure to the program are expected partially on the basis of recent experimental studies demonstrating, and affection by observation of a model. What the model did in these studies had much greater impact on the child's behaviour than what he said. Adult admonitions that sharing was expected or admirable had little effect, but an adult who actually shared or helped another, even while saying that he did not think it is good idea, was imitated.

Another reason for the sex difference may be the predominance of male characters in the media, providing more figures with whom boys can identify. Most current media content reinforces immature aspects of children's thought and behaviour, such as aggressive reaction to frustration, lack of self-control and social stereotyping, rather than enhancing the development of more mature modes of thinking and acting. The potential for more positive socialising effects of the media has been realised in a few television programs, such as "Sesame Street" and "Misterogers' Neighborhood," in which artistic creativity and knowledge about children's development are skillfully combined. Greater publicity and funding have accompanied "Sesame Street," Partly at lest, because it focuses on that current vogue in early education-cognitive skills.

Enhancing cognitive development is an essential and worthy goal, yet it threatens to overshadow social and economical development, especially in educational programs for the disadvantaged. Current educational thinking gives relatively little attention to teaching cooperation, consideration for others, non-violent ways of copying with frustration, and mature modes of moral judgment, to mention only a few specifics. Most children can profit from education in these areas, and disadvantaged children probably have as much need for opportunities to learn interpersonal skills as they do for education in abstract concepts and Standard English. The literature reviewed suggests that the mass media could be used effectively as one tool to provide a social and emotional "Head Start" as well as a cognitive one. It is often said that modern man is in the atomic age intellectually, but his modes of human interaction have advanced little beyond primitive times.

2

Early Childhood Education: Practices and Sources

Art activities are beneficial to children because they contributed to children's capacity to make and understand meaning; education in art should be directed toward this end. Thus, this chapter will focus on research as it applies to the creation of meaning and will take up issues in the development of this capacity, including construction of concepts of materials, of visual properties, of the formation of imagery, and of the meaning of images. Since a number of studies do not fall within this rubric, a *Survey of Other Research* has been included just before the *Conclusion*. Research in art education is comparatively new and suffers from difficulties in examining complex and elusive phenomena; as a consequence, the quality of studies widely. In order to frame the discussion in an historic context we begin with a review of art educational practice over the past century.

In the recent past, working with art materials has been thought therapeutic to the emotional health of young children. It has been valued as a release from anxiety and inhibition and as an appropriate outlet for aggressions and fantasies. Similarly, it is understood to supply adults with insight into the emotions of children and it is thought conducive to the development of creative capacities. Interwoven with these goals has been the belief that both the therapeutic and the creative functions of art will occur best without direction from the teacher. Schaffer-Simmern joins the teacher not to interfere with the natural unfolding of artistic activity. Serious attention to children's art began at the end of the nineteenth century. Numerous descriptive accounts of the developmental changes in drawings were written in biographies of infants by parent-psychologists. These studies established a serious attitude toward children's art work and also set forth a sequence of natural development in drawing that began with scribbles, passed through a phase of schematic work, and achieved more adultlike representations in later childhood.

At the same time that these studies wee taking place, there was a shift in education toward a more child-centered pedagogy. In Germany, Froebel called attention to the natural interests of the child and capitalised specifically on the childs' desire to manipulate materials. There were also art educators such as British, who proposed a curriculum based on the organic evolution of artistic forms from simple to complex, and Cizek, who professed to offer children no instruction until asked, Cizek claimed instead to substitute sympathy and understanding, allowing creative expression to come from within the child. During the same period, John Dewey called attention to the whole child. He theorised that children were organism developing in and through interaction with the environment, and the held that they needed freedom to exercise their intelligence in the environment. The principle of noninterference also received reinforcement from the work of Freud. His *On the Interpretation of Dreams* had been published in 1900, and as the relation between art and unconscious needs and desires was recognised, art came to be seen as an avenue for therapy.

Another important factory contributing to an emphasis on freer forms of artistic activity was the emergence of the Modern movement in art. Expressionism, Surrealism, and Cubism came into being and were recognised as style during this period. Indeed, in 1913 the famous Armory Show held in New York, Chicago and Boston heralded to Americans art as expression, experiment, and individual innovation. These historical trends-the study of child development; he liberalisation of educational practice through the work of Froebel, Cizek, Dewey, and others; the relating of art of unconscious needs by Freud; and the emergence of innovation and expression as explicit values in art-came together in the work of Victor Lowenfeld, an Austrian art educator who came to he United States at the time of Hitler's rise to power in Germany. Lowenfeld was personally affected by the inflexible dogmatism and disregard for individual differences in German educational practices at the time. He believed that such training had made the eventual acceptance of Nazi totalitarianism possible. His book, *Creative and Mental Growth*. Fist published in 1947 proposed freedom for the child, nonintervention by the teacher, respect for the sequence of developmental stages, and mental *health-cum*--creativity as the ultimate goals of art in the schools. Creativity was associated with innovation and was held to be innate, emerging organically with development. The role of the teacher was to keep damaging influences out so that the natural unfolding of creativity would not be stunted or impaired. The drawbacks of

Lowenfeld's program are evident in the light of contemporary developmental psychology, Current theory holds that development is the result of interactions between genetically prompted structures in the child and stimulation from the environment; consequently, children are believed to need stimulation to progress normally. It may be that Lowenfeld believed outside influences would stifle children because he equated children's creative processes with those of adults. However, children's artistic activities differ significantly form those of adults. For children, making art is the creation of order in a relatively limited ad disorganised state of knowledge. With few rules and minimal information children strive to organise and image their thoughts and feelings about the world of experience. Adult artists, working with much more information and many more rules strive to move beyond conventional rules and constraints to imagine new visions or reality. The children's goal is order; the freshness of their work is a sign of their lack of rules as well as their nascent ingenuity in the creation of meaning. Conversely, for artists the goals freshness of vision and the struggle is to achieve subservience of order to freshness of vision. Lowenfeld seems not to have recognised this crucial difference and to have transposed the adult need for freedom form cultural constraints to freedom from culture for children. Apparently, he was unable to imagine how adult artistic influences might beneficially be provided for children. This may be because he had no general theory of cognitive-affective development in art and could not select content from artistic sources in accordance with an organised view of children's developmental needs and abilities. His own discussion of developmental stages in art is limited to a descriptive account of imagery and reference to emotional needs and benefits.

There is little mention of cognitive processes or theory. Furthermore, since he had omitted drawing from observation form his program for young children, the stages he described were based on memory work and offer a restricted picture of children's abilities. His caution is understandable; and, indeed, without a deep understanding of children's artistic processes, teachers may impose on them as she feared. But with the awareness of this problem and more insight into child development, no such negative outcome need occur. This discussion has called into question some current educational beliefs and practices. Among them art that (1) the role of teachers is to help children make images of the sort described by Lowenfeld but otherwise to refrain from intervention; (2) a major purpose of art in the schools is to provide opportunities for uninhibited expression; and (3) children should not be exposed to adult art forms or work from observation. These beliefs and practices are country to the dynamics of child development, and their revision through study of cognitive-affective processes in art in necessary to foster the creation of meaning in art education. The study of meaning creation may fruitfully be approached through the analysis of the processes of symbolisation as discussed in developmental psychology. In order to avoid confusion with more current uses of the worlds symbolisation and representation, it will be helpful to clarify the meanings as used here. Symbolisation is the more general of the two referring to any and all events in which people use some means to call to mind nonpresent persons, objects, or events. Gestures, words, graphic images, play, and dreams are all vehicles of symbolisation.

A symbol is more usually thought of as an image that refers to another entity metaphorically-for example, when a lion is used to denote strength. This form is subsumed, together with all other forms of reference, in the term symbolisation as it will be used here. Representation refers to a limited subsets of visual symbolisation as discussed in developmental psychology. In order to avoid confusion with more current uses of the words symbolisation and representation, it will be helpful to clarify the meanings as used here. Symbolisation is the more general of the two referring to any and all events in which people use some means to call to mind nonpresent persons, objects, or events. Gestures, words, graphic images, play, and dreams are all vehicles of symbolisation. A symbol is more usually thought of as an image that refers to another entity metaphorically-for example, when a lion is used to denote strength. This forms is subsumed, together with all other forms of reference, in the term symbolisation as it will be used here. Representation refers to a limited subset of visual symbolisations in which some physical quality of a symbolising medium is in an isomorphic correspondence with some physical quality of a referent. Thus, in a painting of a tree there is physical correspondence of shapes and colors between tree and painted lines. There are nonobjective as well as objective forms of symbolic reference. In nonobjective symbols, expressive properties of symbols are understood to convey meaning without referring to concrete objects. For example, lines can convey qualities such as speed or uprising movement and emotions such as excitement or depression without depicting objects. The dynamic nature of the process of symbolisation is most powerfully etched in the theory of Western and Kaplan. Their theory proposes that a symbol and the concept of the object to which it refers are created in relation to each other by "forrn-building processes." It is the activity of these form-building processes that brings experience into realisation for children as well as for adults. Symbolisation takes place in several modes; gesture, language, play, and the arts. However, the arts are distinguished from other modes of symbolisation by three significant characteristics. First, in art, deliberate consideration is given to aesthetic and formal qualities. The way in which a symbol is designed is as important as the object or event to which it refers. Second, in a work of art, conscious attention is given to emotional content both by the artist and by the audience.

This is not true in more objective modes of communication. Third, these two attributes are united in a work of art because emotional content its embodied in the formal qualities as well as represented in the imagery. Because of the interplay between through and feeling in form and content, it is possible in the arts to symbolise the complex blend of objective and expressive qualities in the experience of real life. Through art the inner and outer worlds of experience may be brought into relation. Thus, the arts serve a particular psychological function: to capture and embody meanings that bridge thought and feeling. Doyle describe the important role of the medium in the bridging process with admirable clarity. The artist, in fact, every thinker needs such a medium, a vehicle for organising ad thinking about experience. And although some psychologists associate thought with logical operations and abstract verbal generalisation, the artist, thinking in a medium, thinks differently. He thinks forms, and people talking, and images, and rhythms.

When the artist thinks in this way certain so-called logical distinctions disappear-for example, the distinction between intellect and emotion. In life we simultaneously grasp and experience and feel it emotionally; we understand that someone is helping us with no apparent benefit to himself and we feel gratitude. We feel the grayness of the day as rain approaches and feel the melancholy. In a medium, an artist can simultaneously communicate event and feeling. Doyle also refers to the medium as "a kind of reality principle" because its characteristic make specific demands on artists and set up limits against which they must test their dawning conceptualisations. In this respect, materials serve a function similar to that proposed by Erikson for the rules or limits in play. These, he says, provide the structure for "leeway" in play so that the "free" experimentation that develops mastery can take place. In the visual arts, the physical and visual properties of materials provide structure and anchor the form-building process in the concrete.

Three different components of knowledge are used in forming a symbol: the symboliser's known ledge of the material, of the referent, and of the possible modes of correspondence between them. What finally appears in the symbol is a selection from the sum total of information the symbol maker has about the referent and about the material. This selection is based on the symbol maker's understanding of how the two may be related as well as factors relating to the symbol maker's personal and immediate intention. Thus, in order to understand any given symbol one must consider all three components of the process; and to understand children's symbolisation, it is necessary to study the development of all three components. Better understanding of the development of the three components of symbolisation would enable teachers to design appropriate curricula using a full range of resources. It would also enable them to plan lessons and curricula that engage in the creation of the most substantive sorts of meaning from the point of view of the child. Several comprehensive studies cover the first years of artistic activity during which children come to understand the nature of materials. Those of Biber Kellogg and smith are based on collections of spontaneous drawings and paintings. Biber offer's careful analysis of the characteristic of children's drawings in relation to cognitive and affective development; Kellogg provides a classification system of typical configurations; and Smith traces the evolution of visual concepts and includes step-by-step process records of paintings and drawings. There is one full-length case study on an individual child; Arnheim discusses the period theoretically. The account that follows draws on all these sources generally but relies most specifically on Smith.

The influence of a material of the form of the symbol has been a major point for a umber of authors. These investigators have emphasised the fact that a given material elicits and also limits the content of a symbol; some have discussed the child's gradual acquisition of information about materials, but here has been relatively little recognition that it is necessary for children to lean the nature of material before they can use them in symbols. Works of art are made of substances manipulated into patterns of lines, colors, and shapes. In order to arrange a material into such patterns, it is necessary to understand its physical properties, its visual properties, and the performatory actions of hand and eye that produce such patterns. Perceptual response to visual properties such as shape an color is present very early. By the end of the first year of life, sensory response is much like that of children's understandings of such stimuli. However, the ability to respond to visual configurations, as for example a straight line, does not make it possible to produce controlled versions of them, as children's scribbles and copying problems make clear. Nor can we attribute the disorderly appearance of these early efforts to the child's limited motor skills; the drawings would be more random if they were the product of poor control.

It seems more likely that in the beginning, children lack the necessary concepts of physical c and visual properties to give direction to their hands. This interpretation is suggested by the logic of the sequence in which their abilities emerge. As children grow their work demonstrates an orderly progression of visual properties from simple to ever more complex. In the beginning, with no concepts of the possible visible consequences, children move arm and hand in reflexlike motoric rhythms. These movements produce characteristic forms in the material which over time, the child begins to recognise and differentiate. Piaget and Inhelder suggest that the origin of drawing is the rhythmic pattern of the child's undifferentiated state, the fundamental elements of drawing from which more complex concepts will be developed. Smith traces the evolution of the concepts of line, shape, and picture space in three to five-year-old. Lines begin as traces of rhythmic zigzag movements, as noted by Piaget and

Inhelder; thereafter, children master, in order, discontinuity versus continuity, straightens versus curvedness, changes in direction, orientation, and intersection, thus becoming able to control line on paper. In the course of this evolution, and early capacity to produce vertical lines was noted. Connolly and Elliott report a greater proportion of vertical lines in spontaneous easel paintings of children whose mean age is four.

However, Gesell and Ames found that children of eighteen months can copy vertical lines. Apparently children's motor skills are sufficient for copying verticals at eighteen months, but their conceptual skills are not sufficient for producing them without prompting until later. Construction of the concept of graphic verticals may depend on body factors and also on the coordination of the orientation of line within the axes-frame of the paper space. A further extension of these vertical and horizontal coordinations may be the child's preference for perpendicular angles. The capacity to produce controlled shapes emerges form the capacity to produce controlled lined. Children of three and four first create rectangular shapes by drawing a set of parallel verticals and then adding a set of parallel horizontals to them. Only later do they draw a continuous pathway around the perimeter of the shape. Spielman reasons that children's first lines are understood by them as autonomous entities and that when used to form a shape, they lose their autonomy.

Thus, the child requires more time to develop the capacity to draw controlled shapes with a continuous line. Eventually, children construct a complement of visual concepts of line, space, shape, and color that make it possible for them to create organised designs of considerable complexity. It is assumed that the necessary physical concepts of materials are constructed at the same time.

The role of motor activity in the construction of both these sets of concepts would be central in the theory of Piaget. Whatever role it does in face play, it is clear that children teach themselves the performance skills and motor sequences required to create controlled forms of visual graphic elements through manipulative experimentation with materials. Children come to know the different capacities of materials but they also come to generalise properties of materials that are not medium-specific. They are more likely to discover these similarities and differences because their initial movements with each material are very similar. However, because of the different physical and visual properties of each material, similar movements produce different results. Repeated back and forth motions produce patches of color in paint, tangled lines in crayon, and coils or balls in clay. Thus, manipulation leads to both differentiation and generalisation of properties may be seen in other media. Golomb writes of development in the use of playdough as well as drawing.

It is essential to the creation of meaning with materials for the child to develop a deep and rich understanding of the physical and visual properties of materials. In order for this to take place, opportunities for experimentation with appropriate materials over sufficient time are necessary. More empirical research is needed to determine clearly the evolution of the capacity to produce basic visual elements and also to combine them in designs.

The development of an understanding of the physical and visual properties of materials occupies the child's first several years of working with materials. Sometime during the third or fourth year after the child is knowledgeable about materials, the innate capacity for symbolisation begins to emerge in the use of materials, and another dimension of expression is added to children's work. Although the capacity for symbolisation is first evidence during the second year beginning with gestured imitations, it evolves rapidly to include other forms including language and play. Nevertheless, the representational shaping of art materials begins considerable later, during the third and fourth years following the development of basic understanding of materials. Werner and Kaplan hold that the form a symbol takes is the consequence of the maker's conception of the material, the referent, and of the possible correspondence derive form objective similarities familiar to adult but also from another less familiar mode of correspondence based on physiognomic perception. Werner proposed that we have a set of perceptions that respond to expressive characteristics in phenomena. He called this mode of perception physiognomic and described it as more dependent on physical sensation and emotion than on logic. It is natural to young children, available to adults, and much used by artists. Through it, nonobjective imaginary is perceived as expressing emotions and concepts, objective imagery is given emotional force, and composition is used to convey meaning. Through it, we may perceive lines as sad, trees as suffering, and compositions as turbulent. Some characteristics of children's drawings based on physiognomic perception make them difficult for adults to understand; the objective contours of shapes may be ignored and objects may be rendered in simple circles or lines; spatial relationships are simplified and based on topological concepts; movement is often used as feature of correspondence. In addition, the images of children offer grew correspondences while those of adults are redundant, offering multiple cues from lines, spaces, color, and spatial arrangements. For example, a child may call a vertical line "a tall building". In this example, verticality and relative length are they only correspondences the child feels are necessary. Thus, children create sparse images using expressive features, such as movement in line for correspondence, and omitting more objective geometric properties of shape and spatial arrangement.

However, difficult it may be to decode individual configurations, these images in particular deserve serious study, for they embody the foundation of expression in art. in their fusion of form and content, of expressive and objective correspondences, resides the germ of all later creations of meaning and the bridging of thought and feeling through visual means. Children often begin symbolising by naming configurations they have already made. In this proto-symbolic activity, the child's choice of referent is prompted by the configuration of the finished drawing. As a consequence, the choice of referents reflects children's interpretations of properties in the material more than it does their need to present a particular theme. There is an interesting consequence of the influence of materials on the choice of referents at this time. Since different materials have different properties, typical referents identified by young children differ from material to material. In paint, frequently named referents are smoke, rain, and fire;

those in clay are food in various forms; and those in blocks are buildings and portable objects. Names are often prompted by favorite design configurations. For example, a circle with radiating lines is a common design. It combines a number of visual concepts the child has recently learned, including straight and curved lines, enclosure, spacing at regular intervals along a line, orientation of lines, joining of lines at perpendicular angles, and so forth. When beginning to symbolise, the child often calls this configurations "a spider". Physciognomic perception is involved in this creation of a relationship between the lines and the child's conception of a spider. It involves affect in that spiders are frightening and lines that poke or just spider is perceived with global simplicity as a mass in the middle of the many radiating lines.

A common early planned symbol it that of "a man" or "a person," and a common from of it is the so-called tadpole man, that is, a configuration composed simply of a circle with two descending lines. Inside the circle there are usually other circles or lines standing for eyes, nose, and mouth. There is no trunk depicted in the drawing and a number of explanations have been offered for this omission. Arnheim and Golomb consider that the circle represents head and body in one shape, standing symmetrically for the total figure. Piaget and Inhelder, citing Luquet, hold that the trunk is omitted because of the child's inability to synthesise. Freeman suggests that the head-legs con-figuration may be the result of an end-anchoring memory effect. Kellogg and Smith refer to the influence of the child's prior knowledge of circular designs on the configuration. Goodnow studies the influence of the children's rules of sequencing and layout. Werner attributes the large size of faces in general to emotional perspective, that is, emphasis on features with emotional salience. The pattern of this group of interpretations in suggestive. One group of observers focuses on the child's conception of the referent; another, on the child's conception of the material, and another, on the ode of correspondence between material and referent.

The most penetrating explanation will probably be found in an interpretation that takes each of the three components of symbol formation into account. In general, the rules of relationship between materials and referent shift with development from expressive and simplified relationships to ever more differentiated objective and conceptual relationships. The shift to more conceptual relationships is particularly evident in the representation of the three-dimensional world on the two-dimensional surface. Studies record the gradual introduction of occlusion, vertical positioning, and obliques to indicate recession into space in drawing; but specific rules of correspondence are still to be identified.

The shift from simple to more complex rules of representations is paralleled by the child's growing awareness of modes of correspondences. Korzenik studied the child's gradual recognition of the necessity for communicative imagery. Children of five blame any lack of understanding on the viewer, while older children recognise themselves as responsible for making the image comprehensible. Elkind also reports on the development of metasymbolic awareness. Research is needed to clarify these aspects of correspondence and to examine other areas of correspondence as well. Among these is correspondence in three dimensional media and how expressive correspondences continue to be used and elaborated in older children. It is important to attend to the child's gradually evolving understanding of experiences of objects and events. This constitutes the reservoir of information about referents upon which the child draws in forming a symbol. Here particularly, it is important to attend to the child's evolving understanding of what constitutes an appropriate referent for an image. For example, the child to five to seven may understand the act of representation as the depiction of a generic form rather than of an individual object, and thus choose salient parts for their ability to offer categorical definition.

Children's use of simple categorical thought during this age span has been observed in a variety of symbolic modes. If in their early planned representations children have in mind an illustration of a generic car, house, or tree, that might account in part for some of the simplicity of these configurations. Certainly, it is true that there is a developmental shift from representation of basic types such as a person to representation of more differentiated types such as a little girl. Later, children come to add individual objects to their array of possible referents for images. If this progression is the result of changing definitions of an acceptable referent, then the attitude educators have had toward early so-called stereotypes needs to be revised. Rand and Wagner, tracking developmental change in children's representations of a motivated act, observe a similar sequence and note that it is the adult finally who sees the general in the specific. A charming example of changes in the definition of the referents offered by S. Fein. Here, a pictorial record of one child's horse drawing from earliest representations of essential horseness to adolescent consideration of the social context is offered. Children's development of the concept of space has received a great deal of attention, and the theme of perspective taking in particular has been much studied.

This topic is of interest in relation to children's ability to use the convention of perspective. The research derives from a particular study carried out by Piaget and Inhelder in which children, looking at a model of three mountains, were asked to identify viewpoints other than their own. The Piagetian study found that children of six to eight choose their own for all viewpoints, while children of nine to ten distinguish those of others. Piaget and Inhelder suggest that egocentrism declines as the result of internal coordination of all possible viewpoints and that one consequence of this coordination is older children's ability to use the rules of perspective.

However, subsequent studies have challenged the Piagetian account. Some have considered social influences and some, the rotation of the display rather than the subject. Many of these report fewer egocentric errors from younger children than did the Piagetian study. The question of children's perspective-talking ability and its relation to drawing is unresolved and needs further study. More generally, we may conclude that conscientious assessment of art forms must take into account the child's changing conceptualisation of each of the three components of symbolisation. This is true for researchers as it is for teachers. Recognition that a number of factors impinge on the representational process is growing, and many observers are questioning the practice of interpreting art products as indicators of any one factor but the three components of symbolisation deserve much more recognition. Several other factors may need attention as well. These are central processes, emotional status, performatory processes, and the development of the child's capacity to respond to works of art. It is to the consideration of these factors associated with symbolisation that I now turn.

There may be a central symbolising function. While the presence and nature of such a function is yet to be determined, the importance of considering such a possibility is underscored by observations of the unlikely ability of the blind to make simple drawings. If those who have no visual experience of objects or images can make rudimentary drawings, it may be that there are general capacities fro making symbolic correspondences buried deep in the human mind.

The role of memory has been largely disregarded in the children's art literature. It has been assumed that there is no significant difference in young children's work made from memory or from observation, because children at five, six, and seven seem to ignore the scene in front of them. Goodenough and Eng express this conviction and cite a study by Kershensteiner in which young children, when asked to draw a schoolmate, drew other poses in addition to the one before them. However, several recent studies put this assumption to question. Children drawing from observation have been found to produce more articulate contours, to include ore details, and to use occlusion at a younger age. Furthermore, when assisted in the recall of details by dictation, children's representations are more detailed and well integrated. Thus, some simplifications in children's art may reflect difficulties in accessing from memory.

The processes lived in producing appropriate

hand movements also deserve more attention. Olson has given particular attention to the problem of performance and Rand has examined task analysis, motor skills, and motor training in drawing. Studies in which figures are assembled from provided parts indicate greater ability to include parts and to relate parts to the whole. Goodnow has carried out a particularly fruitful series of studies on children's sequencing, economy of means, and rules of layout. Others who have looked at sequencing in drawing are Ames, Freeman, and Smith.

Children's art is often used as means of personality assessment and diagnosis. However, more research on the role of needs and emotions in the formation of symbols by normal children is needed. A better understanding of the interplay of cognitive and affective factors in the forming of children's imagery would offer a more well-balanced, thorough, and comprehensive view of what constitutes normal expression of emotions in art. This review of factors influencing graphic symbolisation has included a wide range of issues including central processing, performatory processing, emotional status, and the three components of symbol formation. The error of attributing any feature. As research continues, one can only hope that more precise means of studying relevant influences and their interactions will be found.

Interest in children's responses to works of are has been growing for some time. Much of it reports children's art preferences based on criteria such as color and subject matter. Children's increasing preference for realism is another frequent observation. Developmental stages of aesthetic experience based on experimental data have also been formulated. In yet other studies it is reported that preference for complexity increases with age ad do comprehension of style and aesthetic principles. Gardne, Winner, and Kircher asked children questions relating to artistic training, media, display, formal properties, and the sources of works of art. They report the relative inaccuracy of younger children's replies. A related area of investigation is picture perception.

Research on children's responses to art has much helpful information to offer teachers. It is essential in educating children to understand artistic meaning to provide them lessons and curricula must be designed. Teachers need to know much more about the aesthetic understandings and interests of children and to present much more of the world of fine arts to them.

Several authors offer reviews of research in the context of other topics: Gardner in an analysis of development across the arts; Harris in a survey of research in drawing and the Draw-A-Man-Test; and Lark-Horovitz, Lewis, and Luca in a general survey of research in children's art.

Current research has begun to identify cognitive benefits to children resulting from participation in the arts. Ives and Pond, in reviewing this material cite studies of improvements in cognitive abilities after children engage in activities including fantasy and dramatic play. They also discuss a renewed interest in mental imagery and its functional effect in problem solving. In addition, Greenfield and others have found parallels between some children's manipulative activities and other cognitive task. These studies point to the intellectual as well as the affective significance of art activities and underscore the need for art in education.

There is a glaring and puzzling lack of research in the areas of special needs and disadvantaged children. Among the few studies on special needs children are reports on leaning disabled children by Walker and development of representation in retardates by Golomb and Barr-Grossman; a case study of a very atypical autistic girl by Selfe;' and a diagnosis and remediation program proposed by Gair. In the area of the disadvantaged, Eisner reports on drawing abilities; Castrup, Ain, and Scott offer an art skills instrument for inner city and suburban preschoolers; Renick reports on an assessment of reasoning and perception in black and white children' and Mills offers a study of the effect of an art program on the reading scores of rural children. There is a pressing need for more extensive study of the art of special needs and disadvantaged children.

Rather more attention has been give to evaluation of teaching strategies. Various studies examine the effects on children's art of perceptual and perceptual-motor training, enriched environment, verbal focusing and reinforcement, and children's critical comparisons between their own or their own and other children's drawings. Another group of studies discuss copying and instruction versus drawn examples in teaching drawing.

The rationale presented for this shift begins with the understanding that mankind is fundamentally symbol-making; that the invention of symbols is natural and yet a source of great pleasure and satisfaction: that through symbols, experience is clarified and shared. The arts are seen as a very much form of symbol making because in them it is possible to bridge thought and feeling and thus portray the rich amalgam of ideas and emotions with which we experience life. A number of consequences for education from this view of art. Among them is the belief that children will gain the most benefit from art programs designed to enhance their capacity to create meaning with visual materials and that this may best be approached by structuring curricula around the three components of symbol formation; concepts of the material, of the referent, and of the modes of correspondence between them.

The visual arts are a particularly appropriate means of expression for young children because art materials are concrete, allowing for direct manipulation and immediate feedback. However, to achieve the most from working with them it is important for children to conceptualise a fully as possible their physical, visual, and expressive properties. To plan for this, teachers need to understand the development of these concepts from their origin in motoric activities to their use in objective and nonobjective forms of symbolisation, Attention to conceptualisation of referents is also required.

Teachers need to help children select developmentally appropriate objects and events as subjects and to help them expand their range of responses to these experiences. Direct as well as indirect experiences of objects, events, and works of art are needed in the classroom. The parallel development of children's objective and expressive modes of correspondence requires particular emphasis. These two modes of symbolisation emerge in a fused state, and they become differentiated, they interact in changing patterns. This interaction is central to the creation of meaning in art and deserves much more attention form researcher and teacher alike. Children's changing concepts of what constitutes an appropriate referent for an image is another important consideration. More accurate knowledge about this, together with more accurate knowledge of how children believe it possible to relate lines, shapes, and colors to such a referent will make it possible for teachers to offer developmentally relevant assistance in the process of forming symbols rather than to avoid this for fear imposing adult modes of correspondence on children. More research is needed that is sensitive to the complex interplay of forces influencing research is needed that is sensitive to the complex interplay of forces influencing the forms of imagery. Information from research will make it possible for teachers to be more active in helping children in work with materials and, in addition, it will help them offer adult works of art to children with more assurance and success. With the creation of meaning as a goal and attention to children's cognitive-affective development as safeguard, far more comprehensive and substantive art programs are possible.

Children can be offered information and experience of the everyday world and of art without harm if these are selected and presented with respect for the children's growing capacities and individual differences. Through more substantive programs, children can be helped to use a broader range of possibilities in the bridging of thought and feeling and of fantasy and reality. Teaching can then be an invitation to full participation in communication and the creation of meaning through art.

3

Development of Early Childhood

A theory of development is not the same as a theory of practice, but the two types of theories interact with each other in provocative ways. In this chapter, we will discuss three developmental theories with respect to implications for a theory of practice. The theories we have chosen for discussion are derived from Bowlby's work on attachment.

Berlyne's on arousal, and Piaget's on mastery and assimilation. Our purpose is not to review the extensive literature these theories have yielded, but rather to select issues that illustrate the relationship between theories of development and theories of practice. Before we discuss these theories, some general observations about theories of development and theories of practice are in order.

Quite generally, theories of development and practice differ in their orientation to the developing individual. The orientation of practice is necessarily activist. It assumes that some aspects of behaviour or some types of knowledge are more or less desirable than others. A corollary is that these require certain environmental conditions which a skilled practitioner can bring about. Should children know how to fight, read, think, imagine, or love? If the answer is "yes", the task of a theory of practice is to describe what a practitioner must do to cultivate that know-how. By contrast, a theory of development is passivist in orientation.

The core assumption is that behaviour changes as a function of encounters present in most environments. Suppose a behaviour ordinarily increases and then decreases during the early years. In explaining this pattern of change, the theory might state that the increase in crying is a by-product of the child's social awareness, a welcome mark of growing maturity. True, the intensity of distress may be related to the child's previous experiences or to the setting in which separation is occurring.

A theory of development will offer general statements identifying experimental and setting factors and why they work the way they do. It will not offer principles for modifying or generating these factors. These theories differ in other ways as well. Theories of development are universalistic rather than particularistic, and, with respect to environmental forces, they are minimalist rather than maximalist. By the former, we mean that theories of development describe what is considered the "normal" course of growth and change. Even when developmental theories expand to consider individual differences, they deal with types of individuals and situations rather than with a particular individual at a particular moment in time. By the latter, we mean that developmental theories tend to view the environment as a set of minimal core features, the presence of which is necessary for development to occur. In developmental theories, the environment enters into serious theoretical discussions when it fail to provide the minimum support needed for growth. Even in the study of individual differences, the goal of development theory is to specify the minimum band of environmental variation required to produce a given individual variation. By contrast, a theory of practice is concerned with the practitioner's perception of particular individuals.

More important in view of its activist orientation, a theory of practice is concerned with maximising beneficial environmental variation. One goal of such a theory is to formulate strategies for constructing. environments that ensure the greatest beneficial impact on the greatest number of individuals. Finally, a theory of development views the changing individuals as a product of the multiple practices of multiple practitioners. By contrast, a theory of practice adopts the perspective of one type of practitioners, and this perspective defines a theory of teaching, parenting, or policy making.

The theory builds on what is known about the child, but it uses only that part which pertains to the environmental conditions controlled by the practitioner of interest in the theory. It is in this respect that a theory of practice may have its most significant impact on a theory of development. A theory of practice must inevitably specify the realisable context in which development occurs. Although developmental theorists have recently called for an "ecology of child development", the emergence of useful ecological constructs may be dependent on the formulation of theories capable of providing rules for producing developmentally consequential contexts. The maximalist orientation of a theory of practice requires far more information about environmental arrangements than theories of development typically provide.

If the task of a theory of practice is to construct rules for generating realisable arrangements outcomes, a theory of practice may need to map the malleability of the environment in which children are reared. John Bowlby's attachment theory is a useful beginning point for a discussion of the interplay between theories of development and practice. Although it serves to underscore the importance of care-giving environments for young children, it stops short of adopting an activist orientation and it fails to address issues of central importance in a theory of practice.

The theory's accomplishments and failures nicely illustrate the relationship between a theory of development and a theory of practice as this relationship might be rather than as it is. Formulations developed by Bowlby to account for the growth and maintenance of children's initial social ties have a variety of philosophical roots. His explanation contains stands from ethology, psychoanalysis, control systems theory, and Piaget's structural approach to cognition. The resultant combination can best be described as an evolutionary-ethological model of attachment. Bowlby incorporated the view of attachment as an instinctual, species-characteristic behavioural system. According to this view, human in-fants are born with a predisposition to display various social behaviours such as smiling, sucking, clinging, following, and crying which act as signals bringing the infant into contact with the mother and eliciting nurturant behaviours from her. This evolution of this system of behaviours resulted from its contribution to the survival of the human infant during the long period of relative helplessness. Throughout the first few years of life, the behaviours which make up the attachment "system" undergo change and modification in response to the current situation, past experiences, and the development level of the child.

Control systems theory and the concept of "goal directed" behaviours were adopted by Bowlby to explain the process by which a child comes to employ a variety of strategies to maintain proximity to the mother. Development changes in the system are explained through Piaget's cognitive structural theory. The first stage refers to the period soon after birth when instinctual signals such as eye contact, rooting, and sucking maintain maternal contact. During the second period, the infant learns to orient and signal to one or more discriminated figures. The third stage occurs along with person permanence when the infant becomes capable of internally representing the parent who is not longer in view.

At this point, active behaviours on the part of the child to regain proximity and contact first occur. This stage lasts from around ten months to three or four years of age. Development changes within this stages are marked by the child's gradually increasing ability to maintain elaborated internal representations of the parents during their absence, representations which serve to reduce concern over separation. Also, the child acquires continually more sophisticated signals to obtain the parent's attention. Bowlby characterises the fourth and final stage as a "goal directed partnership." Separations at this stage are less problematical as the child develops the ability to ascribe purpose to the parent's absence and eventual return. Most investigations of attachment have focused on the third phase when the presence of an attachment figure appears critical to the infant's sense of well-being. The child at this stage has been described as using this figure-whether mother, father, or regular caregiver-as a secure base from which to launch exploratory forays into the environment.

Observing children's behaviour

To picture the developmental process, one can imagine a circle around the child and mother. Under stress the circle becomes smaller and the child moves closer to the mother. Older children's circles become much larger as they use distal signals to "check in." Under stress the circle may contract but not as severely as before. Thus, as long as the child can explore the environment. Anderson described this behaviour in one-and two-year-olds at play in the park. Children would wander from the mother as they became absorbed with toys or other children. Once a certain distance was exceeded, however, the children re-established contact with the mother before returning to play. Attachment research has identified ways in which children use discrete behaviours to signal their need for reassurance and proximity to adults. Sensitive adults observing these behaviours can use them as a guide to the feelings of the child. An understanding of these signals can help a caregiver respond in ways that assist the child in dealing with separations from home and parents. For example, attachment theory suggests that a young child who bursts into tears when the mother enters the center is signaling his need for comfort and contact with the mother, not displeasure or rejection of the classroom teacher. Similarly, a child approaching the teacher to show a toy or standing silently by her side may be displaying variations of the "check in" behaviour described by Anderson. Rather than viewing these behaviours as expressions of excessive dependency, teachers might view them as the child's way of using the teacher as a secure base. The unique aspect of Bowlby's attachment paradigm is its explanatory focus on the development of social ties from the child's point of view.

As a result of the intertwining of ethological and cognitive approaches, observed behaviours of the infant and child can be interpreted as indicators of the child's construction of a social reality. But individual children may differ considerably in the affective aspect of these constructions. Studies of individual differences have identified fairly refined behavioural patterns in children who may require special attention.

Bowlby's attachment theory has provided a fruitful framework for examining the growth of a child's social world. This work has proved useful not only in establishing expected age norms for particular behaviours but in determining patterns of individual differences as well. Perhaps the most productive work of this kind has been carried out by Mary Ainsworth and her colleagues. In a longitudinal study of mothers and infants, home observations were made at three-week intervals over the course of the first year. At one year, a laboratory session was designed to determine the infant's reaction to several short separations from the mother. Qualitative differences in the infant's responses were recorded. The largest group of infants responded to these separations much as attachment theory would predict. They actively engaged the mother on her return, signaling for pickup and comfort if upset, or using distal behaviours if the separation had been less stressful. The next two groups of infants were not as successful in using the mother for comfort and reassurance on her return and generally required a longer period to return to active play.

One group of infants, referred to as "avoidantly attached," responded to reunion by withdrawing or by ignoring the mother. Another group, referred to as "ambivalently attached," responded to reunion with a mixture of both approach and resistant behaviours. Infants in this group displayed the greatest amount of distress over separation but were not comforted by maternal contact. Examination of home observation data indicated qualitative differences in the interactions of the mothers and infants in these groups. During the first year of life, the mothers of ambivalent and avoidant infants had responded less frequently or appropriately to bids for attention from their infants. These individual differences have been found among samples of infants ranging in age from twelve to twenty-four months of age. Moreover, these patterns have been found to be stable over time. But changes from secure to anxious attachment patterns do occur. Interestingly, these are related to stressful changes in the mother's likely to effect interactions with the child.

4

Family Involvement in Early Childhood

About two decades ago, research findings began to confirm the dimensions of the learning risks for children from poor families. Herber, Denver, and Conry documented cumulative decrements in developmental scores of children raised in environments characterised by poverty and low parental education. When maternal IQ was under 80, children's IQ successive ages reveled a progressive drop from 95 on infant tests to about 80 by age four and about 65 by age 14. Herber observed that "the mentally retarded mother residing in the slum creates a special environment for her offspring which is distinctly different from that created by her next-door neighbor of normal intelligence. Ramey and Campbell report scores for children of mothers with a tenth-grade education level and mean IQ of 82. At six, twelve, and eighteen months, the Infant Bayley MDI scores were respectively 102.2, 105.5, and 89.1 Subsequent Stanford-Binet scores at twenty-four and thirty-six months were 80.6 and 84.2. and respectively. Such findings, in conjunction with the civil rights movement for equality of opportunity of all citizens and in concert with a new conceptualisation of the plasticity of early intelligence and its receptivity to environmental nourishment, galvanised energetic public efforts in the decade of the 1960s on behalf of young children. A variety of experimental programs to prevent or to stem intellectual declines among the young who live in poverty environments were funded. Their goals were to enhance children's learning opportunities and chances for school success. Many of the new early childhood education programs proposed and carried out exciting, creative curricula for enriching the learning careers of preschoolers but little attention was given to the influence of what has been called "the hidden curriculum of the home" or to the possible lack of congruence between the efforts of school and home.

Once in school, scores of experimental children declined somewhat. Scores of control youngsters, without previous school experience, began to rise as they, too, now encountered learning opportunities. This pattern of "washout of effect" was found for programs that had been well-staffed and well-run and had adhered to very different theories of child learning. Thus, the pattern was found for Schaefer's home tutorial program for infants. Caldwell's and Richmond's enriched day-care program with high cognitive-language component, and Bereiter and Englemann's group program that emphasised rote drill methods. Follow-up assessments revealed slow erosion of gains after the programs ended.

So persistent was the pattern of failure to maintain IQ and language gains when parental involvement was minimal the child development experts began to rethink their initial premises that early education, by focusing on the child alone. Could compensate for grinding poverty of environment, and that a teacher single-handedly could sustain learning skills of disadvantaged young children without the support and meaningful efforts of those other, far more salient. Teachers back at home-the parents. Schaefer, whose tutors worked one-on-one with toddlers at home until the children were three years old, saw the children's IQ gains erode within three years after the program had ended. Schaefer became convinced that efforts must focus on family-oriented rather than child-centered programs. Schaefer has become an eloquent advocate of family-based programs that can: increase the level of consciousness of parents; make them aware of their importance in their children's lives; help them obtain the information they need; provide the help they need to be more effective with their children; and make them aware of community resources they can use in educating their children.

Hong has suggested that a Parent's "Bill of Rights" should include rights to: knowledge about child development-both emotional and cognitive; observation skills for more effective parenting; alternative strategies for problem prevention and discipline; knowledge about how to use a home for learning experiences for children; language tools and story-reading skills; awareness of being the most important early teachers of their children.

Parental process variables

During the time that preschool programs proliferated, evidence from other research sharpened awareness of the functions of family milieu, socialisation patterns, and socioeconomic conditions that could either support or fail to optimise the growth and educational environment provided for the young.

Process variables refer to intellectual expectations and facilitations of parents and are contrasted with demographic status variables, such as parental education or income. Quality of maternal language, amount of reading and conversation, cultural level of home discussions, and opportunity for the child to learn new words had multiple correlations of 76 and 80 respectively with child intelligence and child achievement. Bradley and Caldwell have also reported impressive correlations of later child IQ and language scores with maternal involvement assessed when the child was two years old.

Appropriate play materials and emotional and verbal responsivity of mother correlated significantly with the child s Stanford. Binet IQ scores at fifty-four months. In summarising such cor-relational studies, Schaefer concluded that "children's test scores were much more related to degree of parent interest than to variations in the quality of schools". Investigations into parent-child exchanges pointed up differences in the abilities of parents to teach their children effectively. Maternal teaching styles varied widely from limited, reactive teaching to effective parental use of suggestions, instructions, modeling, and pointing out critical perceptual cues. Bing emphasised that a democratic home atmosphere as well as maternal acceleration of intellectual achievement was significantly associated with high achievement of children by the fifth grade.

Meticulous research by Hess and Shipman demonstrated differences in maternal teaching strategies of black mothers from different socioeconomic groups. The mothers were asked to teach their four-year-olds how to sort blocks by different attributes and now to create geometric designs with an Etch-A-Sketch toy. The children's task success and IQ could be predicted from maternal teaching behaviors. Low-social-class mothers offered "predetermined solutions and few alternatives for consideration and choices".

A decade later, Bee and colleagues were even more specific in pointing up the social class differences in teaching strategies which support or impede problem-solving success. The middle class mother tended to allow her child to work at his own pace. She offered many general structuring suggestions on how to search for a solution to the problem. She confirmed the child's correct actions so that he could acquire general methods to use in future problem-solving solutions. In contrast, the lower-class mother as a rule did not encourage the child to attend to the basic features of the problem. Her suggestions were highly specific, did not emphasise strategies, and seldom required a reply from the child. By nonverbal intrusions into the child's attempts, she often deprived the child of the opportunity to solve the problem on his own. Research within social class as well as across social class confirmed the crucial nature of family variables in relation to learning progress of children. Resnick found that the amount of conversation in the home, particularly talk directed toward the child's performance on tests. Yet, all families in his project were low-income. Wolf and Dave also related family process variables to child achievement.

Another important research area helped to focus parent involvement efforts more broadly on the total development of the child. Parents are not only the first and most consistently available teachers of their young children, but they also provide the emotional base of security and the motivational roots that nourish exploratory curiosity. Sroufe has reported that securely attached babies, when tested in tod-dlerhood, proved to be more persistent problem solves. They had fewer temper tended to use the parent as a resource to help them solve problems more often than poorly attached children. Thus, if parent involves were to focus only on cognitive aspects of parental teaching, important emotional aspects that support learning might be neglected.

The attachment literature suggests that loving attachment between tutor and child in the family situation sets the occasion for success in attending to learning problems and in consolidating learning experiences in order to solve problems. Even under adverse socioeconomic circumstances, many families give clues for ways in which parent involvement programs can work to support such efforts. Swan and Stavros interviewed parents of low-income black five- and six-year-old children who were effective classroom learners. These children got along well with peers and teachers. They exhibited sustained, self-motivated learning styles. Parents described these children in a very positive and competent light.

The parents fostered independence and encouraged the children to help in the home. They read to their children and talked about a wide range of topics. Positive parenting dimensions were also pinpointed by Carew, Chan, and Halfar. Their naturalistic home observations revealed what family variables correlated with preschooler competence across social class. Suddenly, parent involvement became the indispensable ingredient for engendering optimal learning habits in children and for sustaining the accomplishments of enrichment programs. Some experts concluded that for teachers "to work with children alone is to invite failure and frustration". Others agreed with Chilman that basic income maintenance for poor people "must undergird any program that seeks to deal effectively with poverty and disadvantaged parents and children".

The new thrust to involve parents resulted in federally mandated guidelines for adding a parent involvement component to already existing preschool programs such as Head Start. Whenever an agency provides day care for forty or more children, the Federal interagency Guidelines state that there must be a policy Advisory committee, the composition of which must include not less than 50 percent parents or parent representatives. It is difficult to capture the richness of national effort.

The theory behind home visitation emphasises the continuing impact that a parent can have as a support for and facilitator of the child's learning long after other program supports are terminated. Gordon pioneered the development of the home visitation model, and there are now well over 200 such programs in operation. Gordon envisaged that using trained paraprofessionals, costs could be curtailed and greater empathy and close rapport could be established between the worker and the low-income parents served. Such rapport would enhance the probability that the home visitor would be accepted as a model by the parents. In this project, the primary focus was on teaching the mother learning games during a weekly home visit. The games were based on Piagetian sensory-motor competencies, and a copy of a new game was left in the nome weekly, so that the mother could try out the learning activities whenever she found time. Activities were ordered by area of competence, such as object-permanence games, and were graded by level of difficulty.

Significantly higher general quotients for trained infants were found on the Griffith's Mental Development Scale for 127 trained versus eighty-four control infants. Trained infants also scored significantly higher on personal social skills; hand-eye coordination, and hearing and speech skills. Testing was done between one and two years of age. Lally has documented both the positive strengths and the pitfalls encountered. Some of the problems encountered in training were: difficulty in getting abstract ideas communicated both from training staff to parent educators and from parent educators to mothers; missionary zeal at project commencement which turns to boredom or disillusionment as parents show reluctance to become involved with infants or as infants fail to show rapid intellectual growth; rigid use of the training materials without regard to whether an activity was far above or far below the level of the child's present functioning; reluctance to accept responsibilities for filling out weekly home visit forms and engage in other research data collection and record-keeping efforts; difficulty in accepting freedom to program own time and still be responsible for making all home visits; lack of patience with some families who did not cooperate; resentment that professionals would never understand all the hardships and difficulties that can happen in the field; a desire to work directly with the infants rather than with the mothers.

These problems do not negate the valuable contribution to family involvement that the paraprofessionals made. Their insights into family difficulty and their ability to help some parents feel at ease with and accepting toward the project were often remarkable. Staff problems were dealt with in a variety of ways. Project goals and requirements were dealt with in a variety of switching were used as techniques to increase empathy among paraprofessionals, parents, and professionals.

Gordon's projects established the viability and vigor of the home visitation model and its unique effectiveness when family difficulty with transportation or family reluctance to venture out into "institutional" settings may effectively close out a family from receiving needed service. Home visitation has since become a widespread method of delivery of support for families with the goal of enhancing early development through work with the parent. Home visits may also serve as an adjunct to group services provided primarily for children, as in Head Start programs in many communities.

Honing has summarised the process of home delivery in such programs:

> Through demonstration and practice, tne visitors teach mothers at home how to provide facilitating sensorimotor experiences and language games for their infants. Particularly emphasised are ways in which parents can use daily interactions and caregiving situations with infants to create learning occasions and opportunities. Exercises and games appropriate to the level of development of the baby are taught each

> week; sample fact sheets describing the purpose of each new game and ways to carry out the game are left with mothers. The home visitor focuses on the parent as the important person to work with rather than the baby.

Educational emphasis

Educational programs for parents are often delivered as the integral component for a demonstration research project. The Ypsilanti-Carnegie Infant Education Project demonstrated that a Piagetian-based curriculum could be implemented in the home for low-income parents and their infants in order to enhance the mother's ability to optimise her infant's cognitive development. The goal of Levenstein's Verbal Interaction Project was to prevent educational disadvantage by aiding the two-year-old's early cognitive growth within the family. The mother-child home program was designed to strengthen parents in their conviction and know how to be verbally active teachers of their own toddlers. Levenstein has stressed the importance of training and supervision in the success of her home visitors who are called toy demonstrators. Her program is very cost-effective and securely places responsibility for the learning process with parents not project personnel.

The toy demonstrator's role requires development of a warm relationship with the mother and child, demonstration of verbal stimulation techniques, and the development of maximum mother participation. The toy demonstrator visits each pair twice a week for a half-hour home session. On the first visit each week she brings either a toy or a book which she uses as Verbal Interaction Stimulus material. She introduces the VISM to the child, encouraging it to talk by asking questions, listening to answers, and replying. At the same time, she draws the mother into the session by modeling verbal stimulation techniques, which the mother then imitates. She also encourages the mother to read and play with the child between home sessions. During the year, eleven toys and twelve books are brought to the home to stimulate the mother-child verbal interaction. The model program was run with professionals, and a mean IQ gain of about 17 points was found. The second year, trained paraprofessionals, recipients of the program themselves, were toy demonstrators. Mean IQ gain was 11 points. Replications show that "satisfactory IQ scores were retained by program graduates at least into first grade". At the end of a two-year program for replication, the treated children had a Stanford-Binet score of 104.8 and the control children scored 100.9. These replication results do not suggest as much of the promise as the model program. Possibly because many more of the original families had fathers present in the home and were not on welfare. When the *home visitation model* is used in connection with a research and demonstration project, the process generally includes assessment of family needs, planning, implementation- including role modeling by home visitors for parents on how to teach activities and follow-up procedures.

Sometimes, a home visit includes several aspects. There may be a brief period of prescribed activities aimed at the target child in the family at the same time that the parent in taught a given lesson to be carried out with the child. There may be a period of group activities for other children in the home. Often, there is a period in which the home visitor discusses some of the family's needs as expressed by parents. Child development information, including nutrition and health information, is given. Other information relative to family needs may be supplied, such as how to contact the nearest family planning clinic or how to find low-cost legal services. Forrester describes such a home visitation project, the DARCEE program at George Peabody College. In weekly visits, mothers were provided with the coping skills and assurance they needed to handle the job of being their preschool child's teacher at the end of a year of program participation.

Sometimes, unless certain crucial fundamentals, such as establishing friendly, trusting relations are accomplished, the cognitive aspects of program may prove undeliverable. In Adkin's program in Hawaii, home visitors were to deliver specific language or mathematics curricular lessons for parents to boost the learning of their children who were enrolled in preschool projects emphasising such areas. Many mothers simply were not at home time and again, despite carefully made appointments. The parents assigned to one home visitor, however, were home and available. That worker had made sure that she always took time to listen to family problems and to develop a helpful and friendly relationship with the mothers she served.

There is little sense in assessing the "impact" of a program when most home visits cannot be made. Only as they feel that they are cared about will many families begin to give back the active learning and participation desired. Weikart has pointed out that the home teacher is in a position of low power in the home and must adjust to the pre-eminent position of the parent in her or his own home. Certainly, not all classroom teachers will qualify as home teachers under these conditions.

Clinical and mental health emphasis

Some home visitation projects are more concerned with provision of emotional support and the building of self confidence in families than they are with educational curricula. Van Doorninck reports on a project in which there was an attempt at a parametric variation of the intensity of supportive parent involvement efforts. Pregnant mothers were assigned randomly to one of three treatment groups: (1) routine services of the local health department clinics; (2) home visits weekly through the baby's first birthday by trained visitors; and (3) home visit plus invitations to parent group meetings held every two weeks during the same time period. The purpose of the home visitor was "to provide support to parents, especially mothers, so as to help them cope with their own lives and enhance their abilities to care for their children"

No significant treatment effects were found for measures such as maternal attachment, material perception of self- confidence as a mother, use of community helping service, or mother's educational efforts for herself. The project staff reported that about one-third of the full-treatment group seemed to have little or no overall benefit. They speculated that lack of hard data might be due to the overall excellent level of existing community health services for mothers. The project continued only during the first postnatal year and on the average no more than two home visits of 60 minute each were made per month. Few mothers attended parent group meetings more than a few times. Certainly, sensory-motor tests of infant development rarely reflect rearing milieu differences before one year, the time at which this program was terminated. The lack of any specific educational goals may also be implied in the lack of "hard" effects found. Some families need ling-term efforts of support before family involvement with project goals becomes visible. Sometimes, the effects of parent support may not school difficulties may ensure several years after such supports are withdrawn. Parent involvement may take long commitment to some families. A clinical model which presents no outcome data but is characterised by an interesting theoretical rubric is the UCLA Material Behavior Progression Program. The initial emphasis is on enhancing the quality of mother-infant interaction. This goal requires constant assessment of the mother's feelings toward and skills with the baby. The six levels of Maternal Behavior Progression which the staff or team assists a mother to achieve are: (1) mother enjoys infant; (2) mother is a sensitive observer of her infant; (3) mother engages in a quality and quantity of interaction with her infant that is mutually satisfying and provides opportunity for the development of attachment and the beginning of a system of communication; (4) mother demonstrates an awareness of materials, activities, and experiences suitable for the infant's current stage of development; (5) mother independently generates a wide range of developmentally appropriate experiences, interesting of the infant and adaptive to changing needs. Bromwich objects to parent intervention models that teach a mother how to play with baby. She feels that optimisation of parenting can best be approached by enhancing the mother-infant relationship and quality of interaction at the basic level first and then building maternal confidence level by level. Thus, Bromwich combines clinical plus educational components in a progressive model that evolves as the parent shows signs of being ready for different aspects of this home visitation model.

The emphasis on observation skills is fundamental to a parent program. They ensure project sensitivity to present level of parents understanding and parents' involvement. Many programs are designed to help child-abusing families with home visitation. Child abuse is epidemic at about 2,000 cases per day in the United States. Some projects use two home visitors-one to support the parents and be a parent friend and advocate and another to work on child development activities. Fraiberg used a kitchen therapy intervention model to reach abusive mothers of infants. A skilled, highly trained therapist continues weekly with home visits to build a trusting, caring relation with the neglecting and/or abusing parent. Only as the therapist reaches deeply into the earlier childhood experiences of the young mother do changes occur. As the young mother begins to feel with and for her baby. She may suddenly heat that her baby has been crying for twenty minutes in the loving room; and she may run and pick and comfort the infant.

The home visitation model has proved successful in clinical programs that deal with cases of disturbed parenting and failure-to-thrive babies. A succinct synopsis of a variety if such clinical infant programs, their research goals, and the assessment instruments they are currently using, has been published by the National Center for Clinical Infant Programs.

Many state education departments have worked hard to help teachers of handicapped children look at parents as a sources of stimulation for the children. The most common approach is to have the parent educator come into the home and work with both mothers and their handicapped children. At the University of Wisconsin, counseling as well as practical guidance is provided for parents of blind infants. The home visitor focuses on helping a parent establish a personal relationship with her blind infant and showing the parent how to interest her child in such activities as discovering, grasping objects, and crawling. At the Shield of David program in the Bronx, New York, a home visitor worked with the parent of a retarded two-and-a-half-year old on (1) selecting a more varied diet; (2) suggesting exercises to use with her child on the playground; (3) toilet training; (4) how to associate articles of clothing with specific body parts; and (5) how to make contact with other children.

Frost has commented that members of the family with a child at risk for developmental delay reinforce one another in caregiving attitudes and practices. To be successful, the parents must recognise and accept the child's problems. Helping the mother to learn positive caregiving practices may be less important for what it does for the handicapped child than what it does for the parent. Home-centered training for handicapped or retarded children does not divorce the child from his strongest emotional ties and his most diverse models-the family members. Nor is there any problem of "transfer of training" from an institutional setting to the home. Frost reports that "researchers are still unsure about persisting effects of long-term intervention. Short-term effects are positive and significant." The Wisconsin Portage Project provides parents with activities for multihandicapped preschoolers. Most of the families served live in rural areas so that the home visitation model is more feasible and useful. Parents are taught how to write a behavioral prescription and how to keep daily frequency records of behaviours being learned. They are taught what to teach, what to reinforce, and how to shape behaviors through the technique of initially providing and then "fading out" reinforcements. Each child is assigned individual weekly goals which can be achieved within the week regardless of severity of handicap. The parent is left with written materials and encouraged to carry out each activity several times daily and record what happens.

Possible ethical problems

Levenstein has analysed ethical problems of the home-based intervention model. Because home visitors are generally so strongly and lovingly committed to their work, it may be difficult for a family to think of a reason to resist participation. Also, the degree to which confidentiality about family matters as well as minimal intrusiveness into family privacy can be managed many be problematic. Skill mismatch may occur when family life-styles or problems require more knowledge and ability than a home visitor can provide. The right to worker acknowledgment of a need for further help or professional adjunct services may be a healthy item for a home-based program to keep in mind. The most comprehensive home visitation model, Home Start, was launched as an alternative to provision of Head Start services through group child care. The objectives of the Home Start program are to strengthen parents' capacity for facilitating the development of other children and for direct supports not only for early childhood education but also foe good nutrition, use of social services, budgeting, use of medical and dental facilities, creation of social networks for families, obtaining scarps and materials so parents can create toys and learning activities, and ways that household activities can be turned into learned games. With Home Start, direct and optional benefits can accrue to all children in the family, not just to the target child of preschool age. Home Start children score comparably with Head Start youngsters, and program costs are about the same. Two of the three federally funded parent Child Development Centers in the United States have also used home teaching as an active aid to program for children. In the New Orleans PCDC, parents are provided with a spiral-bound notebook entitle. "In the Beginning; A Parent Guide of Activities and Experiences from Birth to Six Months".

Simple activities, puzzles in text, easy "tests," and observation activities all help the parent to become a more effective child rearer and teacher. The Houston, Texas, PCDC uses home visitation for the first year of the program in order to build basic trust with the Mexican-American families served. Mothers are offered lessons in English, car-driving, and domestic skills as well as child development. After a year, the children are brought into group care. The home visitation component has served to create a secure base of mutually shared goals in a trusting atmosphere for branching out to other forms of family enrichment for children. Parents in the second year of the program participated daily in classroom activities with their children. In the Birmingham, Alabama, PCDC, mother-child pairs attend the center together. After fifteen months on a part-time basis, the mother becomes eligible for Model Mother status, which means a regular 40-hour work week in the preschool program. Outcomes for the children are significantly positive. Stanford-Binet scores for program boys and girls at four years of age are 99.5 and 104.2, compared with randomly assigned control group boys and girls who score at 85.5 and 90.2, respectively.

The reasons for the movement toward parent involvement are often based on the experiences of dedicated professionals trying to work exclusively with children. Poulton and Poulton found in a poor Yorkshire, England, community, for example, that after the first eighteen months, "a more important factor in early education than curricular design and approaches was the degree of understanding and preparation of parents as educators of their children".

More and more sophisticated ways were found to involve mothers and fathers in the education of their children. These children did better on the English PPVT after one year of such parent involvement. Unless the parents could be shown their educative role with their children, the Poultons found that there was little chance of maintaining any momentum gained through the children's early childhood education experiences. Introductory family visits were very important in establishing trust in a future partnership. Soon parents made arrangements to spend an afternoon once or twice a week at the preschool.

Under the auspices of Dr. Ira Gordon, one of the twenty-one planned variation Follow Through models mandates participation of parents in their children's elementary school classrooms. The Sumber Mobile Preschool Program in Syracuse, New York, is a program in which mothers serve as teachers in their own home with the supervision of a trained teacher. The local teacher chauffeurs a few children from the neighborhood surrounding the local elementary school to the home of a neighborhood mother. Gradually, as toys, activities, concepts of numbers and counting, and taking turns, for example, are modeled by the supervisor, the home mother comes to take over more and more responsibility for teaching activities with the group of preschoolers who attend in her home for a half-day. Gordon and Guinagh's Back Yard Center program had a similar concept. Mothers in whose homes preschool activities occurred for a small group of children were employed as helpers to the backyard center directors. These directors themselves were paraprofessionals who had served earlier as teachers in Gordon's home visitation program.

Juniper Garden Preschool in Kansas City, Missouri, was a token-reinforcement preschool for culturally deprived four-year-olds. With the premise that, in the long run, more child progress could be achieved if parents of the children were involved, the staff began to provide lessons for mothers on how to teach their preschoolers. The thirty mothers chosen were characterised as from "upwardly mobile poverty families." Each mothers was rewarded with dinner ware each week for coming to preschool with her child. Every day, each mother at first retired to a booth with materials to teach her child. Initial findings were that "the mothers were poor teachers. They used almost no praise or approval, and they showed little grasp of the technique of attacking complex problem by starting with its simplest form". Changes in the program were then introduced. The mothers were given instructions on how to start with the simplest tasks. They were to praise a child for each correct response, such as naming an object pictured. Mothers were then paired with children other than their own. Threats to children subsequently decreased. Teachers kept records of when a mother praised. They flashed a red light, mounted where the mother could see it. Mothers were asked to press a foot pedal whenever a child answered a question correctly. After a mother had learned how to praise another child, she again was allowed to work with her own child. Mothers also worked as classroom teachers. In unstructured situations in the classroom, mothers found some difficulty in putting principles of positive reinforcement into practice. Staff continued work with the principle that mothers were to reinforce with attention only tat behavior that they wanted the children to continue. From the beginning to the end of the program, the children's PPVT IQs rose from a mean of 69 to 87.

One of the best known methods of involving parent is in the education of their children is to invite them to parent group meetings, usually at a school which the child attends. Programs which involve parents of preschoolers in groups have sometimes opted for cognitive emphasis, for example, on teaching mothers how to improve children's language skills. Other parent groups have focused on: increasing parental self-awareness; knowledge of ways to motivate children; expression of parental needs; home management skills; making and learning to use inexpensive home learning materials; increasing self-esteem in the family; helping parents acquire job skills.

One of the most widely used models for helping parents use toys to teach their children was created by Nimnicht et al. at the Far West Parent/Child Toy Library Program. Parents are involved in eight two-hour session, usually meeting once a week. Child development topics are discussed and a new toy is introduced at each meeting. The toy as a means to boost children's problem-solving skills in demonstrated, discussed, and illustrated in films. Parents at the group meeting role-play with each other the many ways they could use a toy to promote thinking and problem solving. They use these ideas later at home with the toy to help the child make discoveries and increase his skills. Stevens has reported that an eleven-week program of small group parent meetings which included toy/book demonstrations and lending produced significant IQ gains for children of project participants. He suggests that the parent consultants would have been even more effective had they provided feed-back to a parent during this or her interaction with a child in the home.

"Teach Your Child to Talk" is a parent group meeting plant to help parents encourage language development from infancy onward through the preschool years. Parent workshops are carefully programmed with slides, cassette-illustrated vocalisation examples, and a manual for workshop leaders. Programs that involve parents in their child's school learning may be particularly crucial for culturally different or non-English-speaking children. A variety of commercial programs exists to establish such linkages between home and school experiences. One such is Amanecer developed in San Antonio, Texas. Based on the theories of Piaget, Montessori, and Maslow, the model was developed as part of the Head Start strategy for Spanish-speaking children. Teachers are helped to initiate parent contracts, plan parent learning activities, organise parent projects, and create a culturally sensitive learning environment. The goal is to increase the process by which parents become valuable resources in planning and implementing the curriculum for young children.

Parent workshops or group meetings are often inaugurated as supportive services to ensure at-home continuity of teaching with the learnings of the child in an educational setting. Karnes and colleagues provided a mothers' group meeting along with an enriched preschool for the children.

However, no significant added effect of the parent group was found beyond score enhancement found for preschool alone. In contrast, Gray has reported encouraging results for mother participation plus child preschool experience. IQs of children whose mothers were into he parent group remained relatively stable after two years: IQs of children with preschool only decreased further during that same time span. Boger and colleagues arranged for groups of mothers to meet in twelve weekly two-hour sessions with their children's teacher in a developmental or structured language workshop or in a placebo group workshop.

The mother who participated in the specific language interaction groups increased their own language skills. Their children also increased in language skills and have a more positive perception of their mother's view of them compared to placebo treatment group children. This program has been replicated with rural as well as urban parents.

"Education for Parenthood" recently has served as a parenting program curriculum for many Head Start project parenting groups. The program provides three learning modules: working with children; seeing development; and family and society. Parents gain insight not only into children's development but also into themselves as learners. Keeping a journal and learning to observe children are program techniques that help sensitise parents to their children. Lane the director of the NICE program in California, was an early believer in the importance of parent participation in the classroom. Lane further advanced the NICE program goal of helping parents to be more effective teachers of their own and others' children by creating training classes taught by the director and staff members of NICE.

The classes met for two hours once a week for fifteen consecutive weeks. Each participant parent was required to spend one day per week at the nursery school trying out ideas discussed in the class. Each parent was require to learn to observe and record the behavior of a child and read the report in class. In addition, parents shared their backgrounds their dreams for their children, feelings about their own childhood, and problems they had with their children and with each other. The parents drew much closer together, although they came from quite different backgrounds. What were the outcomes? Mothers were judged by the staff to be competent enough to operate the school classes one day per week with the assistance of graduate students. Staff used this time for meetings. Several parents developed a degree of competency that qualified them as teacher aides. Parents became involved in assessing the program of the public schools to get to know the types of class programs their preschoolers would soon be entering. Parents developed considerable confidence in their own resources.

Public school systems, too, often use parents as supports for children's learning. The Benton Harbor Area schools in Michigan have formed a home-school-community partnership, in a Title I project called Project Help. This model provides for a group of teachers to design together with parents a series of activities that will work to support children's school learning in their community. Activities are written recipe-style on a single piece of paper. They are short, easy activities that use kitchen items or living room furniture, for example. These lessons build on school learnings. There are special advantages to the model when parents participate creatively in planning for experiences in the schools in which their children are already enrolled.

As parents learn early education skills, they must examine their goals and values concerning children in order to develop curriculum, select facilities and equipment, and even hire teachers. Also, "the opportunity to meet and share experiences with other mothers in similar situations provides parents with social contact, emotional support, intellectual stimulation,........and a sense of fulfillment and self-esteem to counteract the physical and psychological isolation frequently experienced by mothers".

In Heber's program in Milwaukee, the parent involvement component consisted carefully supervised on-the-job training experiences in laundry and dietician aide work. Parent group meetings helped to build self-confidence as these mothers of low IQ and low incomes struggled with each others help as well as with training to increase job and communication skills. Parent education groups are often active in programs for handicapped children. Methods of encouraging parents to attend meetings include providing transportation, paying for baby-sitters, writing or calling parents in advance of meeting, and arranging small groups for those who seem uncomfortable at larger meetings. Other group techniques include showing parents videotapes of their interactions with their children and encouraging a parent-child album.

The Portland Center for Hearing and Speech taught parents of language-delayed children in weekly sessions. Parents observed their children's language, enrichment program. The meetings had two purposes: (1) to discuss information about home management of communications problems; and (2) to provide emotional support for parents.

The children's progress during their eight-week summer session typically revealed an average of about six to nine months gain in general language functioning and in receptive vocabulary. What parts the parents' efforts played and what part the individualised curriculum played in such gains is not discernible, nor is it known how long these gains lasted. What is clear is that parents rated their own knowledge of factors affecting special problems higher after their group experience. Some programs for handicapped children use a wide variety of parent involvement techniques.

The Delayed Development Project in Stockton, California for example, provides home visitation for children under eighteen months. From that age on, babies are bused into a program with individual therapy and small group activities. Parents spend one morning a week in school with their tots. "Dad's Day" classes are held on Saturdays. Evening group meetings with a psychologist allow parents to support each other as they discuss their fears, hopes, anxieties, and problems. Bricker and Bricker, in their program for integration of Down's Syndrome and normal preschoolers have consistently involved parents in care-giving activities toward behavioral goals. Bassin & Drovetta report that parent-to-parent contact in particularly helpful when trained parents help those who are newly facing the problems that ensue with the birth of a handicapped child. Their St. Louis, Missouri, program trains parents to help each other with jargon-free explanations about disabilities, helpful hints on home training, and assistance in locating community resources.

5

Teenage Parenting: The Problems and the Programs

In 1979, 29 percent of births to white teenagers and 83 percent of births to black teenagers occurred outside of marriage. One of five babies born in the United States today is born to a teenage girl. At Johns Hopkins University, Dr. Hardy and her associates found that among children sixteen years or under who were below grade level in school, 75 percent had teenage mothers. Among children who had started major fires, 70 percent had young mothers. There are about 700 programs around the country that try to help pregnant teenagers and their babies. "Education for Parenthood" was originally designed as a multimedia program to help teenagers learn about children and how to care for them. Badger brought groups of low-income teenage mothers into group meetings in a hospital setting during evenings when the teenagers were not at jobs or continuing their schooling. Her program offered a wide variety of information and skills at levels that these very young mothers can understand. Demonstrations of infant competen-cies, talks on good nutrition and infant care, encouragement of affectionate mother-infant contact were among the activities. Young mothers were challenged when they exhibited attitudes of withdrawal and hopelessness.

Honig noted that Badger's own enthusiasm for positive parenting practices was a major ingredient in encouraging some of these young mothers to become involved with their babies. Many programs for teen parents not only focus on parenting and child development skills, but they also encourage continuation toward a high school diploma by offering special educational programs housed in a building where infant care is also provided. Innovative and flexible programming is needed to deal with the national "epidemic" of teen parenting.

The Family Development Research Program and Children's Center in Syracuse. New York, has tried to actualise an "omnibus model". Paraprofessional home visitors, indigenous to the low-income community, brought nutritional, child development, and child care information to pregnant mothers. After the infant's birth, the family was taught special games to encourage visual alerting, hand-eye coordinations, and vocalisations.

Mothers were encouraged to improve their own and their babies' diets. At six months, infants entered the Children's Center, a developmental day-care program. Families continued to be visited by the Child Development Trainers (CDTs), and parents continued to receive child development information and skills until the child reached school age. Language, sensory-motor, and later proportional games and tasks as well as child-management ideas and techniques were presented. CDTs lent toys and books. They provided information and references to community resources to help with legal aid, health care, housing, food stamps, and other problems. They provided loyal friendships to mothers often beset with severe emotional, sexual, social, and financial crises.

CDTs served as liaison persons between the parent and the center. Complaint department, information clearing house about center activities, escort service for parents visiting the center, participant in parent group monthly discussion meetings, active worker at weekly parent workshops, bearer of special family news a teacher may need to know-all these roles filed by the CDT as her repertoire of family-facilitating skills expanded. CDTs held parent group meetings in homes for those parents who were interests in group discussion about special topics. Topics which parents requested included effective parent participation in the public school after the child entered the school, sexuality and early childhood, and working mothers and young children. The FDRP gave particular attention to the importance of selection, preservice, and in-service training of the home visitors. The paraprofessionals initially underwent eight weeks of training in nutrition, health, interviewing techniques, and games and activities to facilitate early cognitive development.

At forty-eight months, FDRP children were significantly ahead of low-education matched control groups on all seven ITPA language subtests used. By seventy-two months, however, these differences were no longer found. Stanford-Binet mean scores for program children at forty-eight months and seventy-two months were 100 and 109 respectively, compared to 101 and 105 for low-education controls and 136 and 138 for high-education contrast group children. Thus, program children were functioning well in early elementary school grades but they lagged markedly in IQ scores compared to children from intact, college-educated families.

One of the most comprehensive program efforts to involve families of preschoolers in enhancing living and learning conditions for their children is the Child and Family Resource Program (CFRP), a national Head Start demonstration program, which was initially funded in June 1973. CFRP uses Head Start as a base for developing a community-wide service delivery network. A key feature of CFRP programs is flexibility and thoroughness in meeting family and child needs. This individualisation and tailoring of programs to fit each family is a strength that augurs well for the success of CFRP programs. Another feature of CFRP programs is the attempt to involve resources in each community to serve the diagnostic and remediation needs of family members. A third is the provision of continuity of services from the prenatal period through early elementary school years. The fourth objective of CFRP is to enhance an build upon the strengths of the individual family as a child-rearing system with distinct values, culture, and aspirations.

A variety of innovative programs for parents has arisen as parents needs are articulated ever more clearly. Locales and program personnel may be nontraditional. Pediatricians' offices serve as a meeting place for parents as does the storefront "Parent Place" and outpatient waiting rooms of hospital pediatric services. Hot lines provide instant telephone information and comfort to parents who need help in coping with early child rearing and educating. Libraries institute toy and book lending programs. Grass-roots self-help parenting-education groups are being started in many communities by mothers who find they need to learn with each other and share their problems and adventures in child rearing. Programs that dovetail home visits and parenting activities with television programs for children have proved cost-effective and are widely accepted. The Look-At-Me television series highlights discipline, family relationships, child emotions, and how parents can nurture child curiosity and learning. TV guides to stimulate family discussion are available from Prime Time School Television in Chicago. Many publications and audio-visual media are now available as self-help guides for parents. Some materials are designed primarily to help parents develop positive communication systems and loving relationships with children. Examples are books by Bessell and Kelly ad Ginott.

Other packages can be used in parent groups with a leader. Gordon's "Parent Effectiveness Training" is the most famous of these programs. Parents are taught how to use "no lose" problem solving techniques, appropriate "I" and "You" messages, and "Active Listening" to help increase positive family communication. Interviews with parents who have undergone PET reveal way in which the program helped families. The Systematic Parent Effectiveness Training Program teaches parents how to analyse the goals of children's misbehaviors and positive behaviors and to respond in ways to increase the latter. Both the these programs deal more with parent of school-age children.

Some self-help materials are designed for specific parenting groups, such as Spanish-speaking parents or low-literacy parents. New Reader's Press in Syracuse, New York, has parenting materials and activities designed for readers with less than a fifth-grade education.

Shure and Spivack have taken a problem-solving approach to training low-income parents and teachers of inner-city children to teach the children to generate solutions to interpersonal problems and to foresee consequences of their own behaviors in such a way that the children can make better adjustments: "To date, the most powerful ICPS mediator in young children appears to be the ability to conceptualise multiple solutions to interpersonal problems and, secondarily, the ability to anticipate the consequences of acts"

These findings continued to hold up in comparison to control children one year later. The authors report that those mothers who consistently applied problem-solving techniques when real-life problems arose had children who most improved in ICPS thinking skills and subsequent behavioral adjustment. The kinds of dialogues and scripts that are taught, of course, require that parents acquire new thinking skills of their own. "Training parents to think through solutions to interpersonal problems and to anticipate the consequences of acts helps them appreciate the very thinking process they in turn learn to transmit to their children".

6 Early Childhood Education

A Curriculum model provides an ideal representation of the essential philosophical, administrative, and pedagogical components of a grand education plan. It constitutes a coherent, internally consistent description of the theoretical premises, administrative policies, and instructional procedures presumed valid for achieving preferential educational outcomes. Ultimately, this abstraction can serve as the basis for educational decision making. As decisions are translated into action, we can speak of model implementation, thus enabling the empirical study of models. This chapter has two related purposes. The first is to explore major components or characteristics of early childhood education models with reference to selected conceptual issues that permeate the literature of models development. Second, various concepts and issues about model analysis and evaluation are reviewed, with emphasis upon recent developments important for improved evaluation practice.

Curriculum models have appeared in one form or another since the advent of formal education for young children. But focus upon the utility of early education curriculum models has sharpened considerable in recent years. Perhaps the most notable force in this sharpening process is the planned Variation experiment first integrated into Project follow Through, later extended on a limited basis to Project Head Start. Selected educational authorities were encouraged to propose conceptual alternative for controlled application in educational settings for children ages four to eight.

The result was a widely ranging set of curricular activities and instructional strategies to operationalise preferred philosophies or theories of child development, learning, and education. At its zenith, as many as twenty-two alternative education plans, called models, were considered for Planned Variation. Implicit in this thrust to develop, implement, and evaluate models were two fundamental assumptions: no one best way exist to educate all children in all social contexts, and different curriculum models are variously well suited for different children in different social contexts. This move to develop alternative curriculum models was consistent with the value of pluralism in education, conceivably to provide the citizenry with choices among legitimate and comparable educational designs. Serious students of early childhood education theory and practice will note many important questions about the alternative models ideal, three of which are addressed here.

The first question concerns model building-that is, which model characteristics or components are functional and relevant as a framework for developing curriculum models in the original sense? Once determined and used for model building, these characteristics or components should be further useful for the comparative analysis of alternative models. Such analysis normally will concern a specification of similarities and differences among models at theoretical-descriptive level.

As for similarities, a prime issue is the extent to which models agree upon certain fundamentals even though these models may emerge from diverse theoretical wellsprings and represent "different roads to Rome". Authentication of similarities may result in the identification of a basic core of principles and conditions: to represent the best of educational thought about early childhood curricula, and to serve as the point of departure for the creation of new curriculum models. A parallel issue is the extent to which model rationales may differ in substance or design. From these differences will flow implications about children's educational welfare, cost to society, suitability to various social contexts, and so on. Differences among early educational curriculum models are certain to reflect value commitments about what is more or less important for young children and their families.

Presumably, these differential commitments will affect educational practices and, in turn, educational outcomes. It is incumbent upon model builders clearly to identify these commitments at the theoretical-descriptive level so that analysts and consumers can determine distinctiveness. A second major question about curriculum models goes beyond a conceptual analysis of similarities and differences at the theoretical-descriptive level. To wit, how clearly are these theoretical model similarities and differences revealed in actual educational practices? It is one thing to state distinctive curriculum components on paper; to validate such components by way of empirical observation is quite another. Validation requires a set of procedures for measuring model implementation, often referred to as process evaluation Process evaluation involves an assessment of the presence and merit of program components antecedent to or theoretically functional for attaining model objectives. The third major question about curriculum models is to what extent various models when implemented competently, are effective in producing their intended educational outcomes? This question usually draws attention first to any changes in children's behavior and development that are associated with model implementation.

But outcome assessment will often include the evaluation of changes among teachers, parents, and even community services that follow model implementation. In practice, curriculum model guidelines can vary markedly in criterion-based evaluation. This means that the acid test for model implementation is how well or how completely stated goals and methods of a given model as inherently worthy and evidence can be marshaled to demonstrate the model's capacity to "deliver", it may matter little how the favoured model compares to others. However, many consumers are understandably intrigued by questions about which models are more or less efficient and effective for achieving generic outcomes.

This implicit competitive aspect of model development and implementation may be masked by the idea that different models are more or less effective for different outcomes. So the issue of comparative model effectiveness lingers on. To summarize, a clear conception of model characteristics is relevant for several important tasks. Such characteristics can serve as analytical criteria useful for model selection. Those characteristics also provide a basis from which to plan model improvements and even create new models. An understanding of model characteristics is relevant to educational researchers. Many characteristics can be considered as independent variables to guide model implementation and impact research. Eventually, this research may provide a clearer picture of what model children whose needs and learning styles differ. In fact, research along these lines may disclose that some characteristics have little, if any, bearing on children's educational development while others are critical for this development. As model features are empirically validated., much of the speculation of guesswork about model development and implementation should be reduced, if not eliminated.

A careful examination of the literature suggests that program models can be analyzed for three major categories of program components: theoretical foundations, administrative policies, and curriculum content and methods. In this section, each category of components is explained with reference to illustrate conceptual and evaluation research issues.

Theoretical foundations for curriculum models typically reflect a mix of philosophical and psychological thought about educational aims. This mix will include value statements about the basic purpose(s) of education in concert with assumptions about children's learning and development. Thus, "should's" and "ought's" about education to promote the good life are focal. These statements of good usually link with convictions about what are the essential conditions of learning and development for instructional design.

The interrelationships of educational ideology and psychological theory are at best complex and intricate. At worst, these interrelationships are obscure, confusing, or conspicuously absent. Over time, however, certain bodies of consistent, integrated thought about philosophy and psychology have come to dominate curriculum models for early childhood education. These bodies of thought are identified by various labels, such as the behaviorist, dynamic and constructivist approaches.

Model philosophies and educational aims are diverse, but much of their conceptual diversity can be reduced to a relative emphasis upon one or another of two broad goal orientations for children: to nurture general socialization or to achieve specific learnings, usually in the academic realm. Also associated with this emphasis are differences in interpretation of ideas about education as preparation for the future. One interpretation is a claim that young children's education should be designed on the basis of requisites for success in adult society. Children's momentary or transitory needs and interests are subservient to adult beliefs about what achievements and skills are essential for socio-economic self-sufficiency. Applied to early childhood curriculum models, this view includes support for "continuity in the educational enterprise as it currently exists".

A foremost priority is solving the problem of sequencing preschool educational demands to better prepare children for successive demands in the kindergarten and primary grades. This means that educational planning is essentially a "top down" experience. Broadly defined adult roles and values form the basis of formal K-12 span of educational requirements. Early childhood curricula, as preschool-kindergarten, are conceived to facilitate successful adaptation to existing primary programs, and so on. Although all formal educational programmes are to some extent "preparatory," the issues is one of degree or emphasis. Education as preparation or the future may too easily result in a "Cold storage" concept of learning. Should educators not be forced to justify the worth of learning experiences for children in terms of some projected scholastic or socioeconomic value? It is argued that such thinking diverts attention from young children's interests and unique learning thinking styles, especially as expressed in play. Instead, their uniqueness should be nurtured to stimulate balanced affective and cognitive development. Protagonists for a nurturance view of early education claim that the best insurance for successful adulthood is fully enriched, day-to-day, child-centered experience. From this, children will best develop a secure sense of competence and selfhood. Curriculum planning begins with an analysis of children's developmental characteristics, consistent with their unique needs, interests, and modes of thinking- a "bottom up" design. In this way, a strong foundation for subsequent growth and development is achieved. Concomitantly, ideal early childhood education may promote both social and educational reform. This is because the educational system would accommodate *to* children instead of requiring the conformity dictated by top-down curriculum development.

This philosophical difference in curriculum aims and purposes is paralleled in the fields of developmental psychology: a schism between proponents of "naturalistic, indigenous growth" theories of development and the "cultural competence" or "environmental determination" viewpoint. The schism aggravates contentions about desirable conditions of learning. These contentions, in turn, line to preferences about curriculum methods.

Advocates of the natural growth or maturationsist view argue that the best education will be achieved by providing children with an enriched, begin, accepting, permissive, and relatively informal environment. High value is place upon children's need for creative expression. Through such expression, self-development is best nurtured; developmental or maturational sequences provide whatever cues may be important for realizing individual growth potentials. In contrast, supporters of the "cultural competence" school emphasize more the shaping power of experience and necessity for social adaptation. Systematize and direct tuition thus figure more prominently in socialization practice. Skill achievement. Accordingly, the structure and continuity of environmental events will largely determine children's patterns of learning and development. This schism in thinking about the nature of human development has been adroitly couched in terms of *context-free* versus *context-sensitive* theories of development.

Early childhood educators sympathetic to the universals of child development, especially stage-sequence interpretations from genetic psychology, will claim that basic principles of developmental education apply to all children. These principles should provided the basis for common educational experiences at successive age levels. Though differences in developmental level are carefully accounted for, differences associated with socioeconomic status, racial-ethnic identity, and other demographics do not figure strongly in thinking in about goals or aims. Form this it can be argued that development per se is the fundamental aim of education. Philosophies that are context-specific or context-sensitive will, in contrast, accentuate the role of cultural variables in promoting or impeding children's skills acquisition. Thus, educational aims may emerge from an analysis of any leaning deficiencies allegedly rooted in social background experience. Schism in education philosophy and psychological theory represent, of course, degrees of emphasis, not conceptual dichotomies. Thus, curriculum model philosophy and aims can be viewed in relative position along a given continuum of thought. For example, the applied behavior analysis approach leans more in the direction of a cultural-competence, context-sensitive viewpoint than do constructivist approaches, which have more in common with a natural growth, context-free position. Even, so pure applications of educational philosophy and developmental theory are not easily observed in everyday, practical experience. Theoretically based differences *can* become a reality, however, as indicated by various model demonstration programs and the planned variation experiments within Projects head Start and Follow Through.

Among the clearest theory-based differences are extent of child-ceneterdness in educational planning, nature or type of leaning sequences, account on basic academics, incentive systems, and explicitness in seeking affective outcomes. These differences are generally consistent with values and assumptions of alternative philosophies and theories. However, in the final analysis shorter-term objectives and methods for achieving them seem more vocally disputed among early childhood educators than are longer-range educational aims. In face, efforts to promote unification of purpose have been called for under the banner of social competence.

One's philosophical view of education and human

development is the foremost model component from which statements about curriculum goals, content, and method will emanate. For a conceptual analysis of models, the issue for this component is twofold: comprehensiveness and internal consistency. A comprehensive, internally consistent statement will articulate the theoretical basis from which a model is conceived to clarify the logical interrelationships of philosophy and psychology. It will also clarify assumptions about educational purpose, conditions of human learning, and the nature of human development. It will further show how assumptions are integrated with other basic model components, especially curriculum content and methods. Coherence of philosophy and aims is a matter of both degree and kind. This necessarily requires a careful study of curriculum in concept as well as in implementation. A second major category of curriculum model components concerns policies and procedures for overall program administration or management, In contrast to philosophical discourse about education and child development, specific literature about administrative variables of early education models seems less extensive. Consequently, much information about this topic must be extrapolated from or general educational administration literature. It is perhaps significant that specific administrative concerns are being addressed more and more by early childhood professionals. There seems to be no definitive consensus about how best to categorised administrative policy variables fort the conceptual analysis of curriculum models. Some administrators prefer a human relations approach to administrative policy. Their focus is staff and community involvement for policy development and implementation. Other administrators work form a more technical orientation to management, dealing especially with the economics of a program, including fiscal policy and cost efficiency studies. Still others take an ecological stance, stressing the study of political, sociological, and legal forces that influence or dictate administrative decision making. Acknowledgment of different orientations need not distract attention form the point that administrative variables represent decision-making points about how best to insure the success of an educational program.

Accordingly, it is convenient to group administrative policy variables into three interrelated categories upon which is superimposed a method for establishing program budget. These are policy about personnel, the physical setting for model implementation, and program evaluation. Personnel specifications for early education curriculum models include nature of the population to be served, identification of staff to deliver basic services, and community participation or involvement, especially parents or primary caregivers. Criteria should be present to define pupil eligibility for a given model or population characteristics useful for determining the suitability of a model. These criteria may include age, cultural-linguistic background, socioeconomic status, clinical health status, ethnicity, and even sex. Some models claim their suitability for all children of a particular are group or developmental stage, regardless of cultural background. Others are designed specifically for special populations as, say a bilingual program for limited English-speaking children, In addition. A pupil personal services policy should, address the following topics: health, safety, nutritional standards, individual pupil assessment practices, procedures for reporting pupil progress to parents, referral procedures for children with special problems guarantees for children's rights and general ethical guidelines for program quality. Program staff, a second major category for personnel policy considerations, concerns teachers, aides, administrators and supervisors, and adjunct service personnel.

Minimal staff qualifications, hiring policies, in-service training provisions, staff evaluation procedures, staff pupil ratio designations, grouping practices, and extent of staff involvement in curriculum decision making are common sources of personnel staff variation. To illustrate, one sorely argued difference in early education staff function is the extent to which teachers are trained to implement a fixed or "teacher-proof" curriculum versus developing competence in the management of one that is more fluid. Flexible, informal. Standards or requirements for preserves credentials, staff training, selection, and evaluation will be influenced substantially by one's position on this issue. A third major category of policy considerations deals with forms of community involvement in early education programs.

These forms usually vary according to the age of the children. If a model's major thrust is home-based education, then parental involvement policies-including parent education-are of paramount importance. Strategies for securing involvement can be described along a continuum from none-to-minimal to nearly complete parental control of an educational program. Some models are founded upon principles of parent involvement. Others exclude direct parent participation. Either way, policies can be traced to a model's theoretical foundations and should generate testable assumptions about the relationship of parental involvement to children's developmental education. These policies may also extend to decision making about parent education. Inextricably bound to administrative considerations are physical setting requirements for model implementation. This calls for attention to space equipment needs and their arrangements, juxtaposed with health and safety standards. Existing programs carry remarkably in the degree to which ideal physical rationale.

Well-developed models often provide explicit graphics, as floor plans, to guide appropriate implementation. Minimum square footage for classroom and playground space may also be recommended. These considerations are significant in view of two broader issues about the physical environment for early education: first, *the place* where children's formalized early education is best conducted, and second, *what effects* physical space variables may have on children's behavior. Space considerations are closely bound to time use as well. Time use-meaning allotments for specific learning activities- anticipates a forth coming discussion about curriculum methods. But administrative policy issues are also involved in decision labour full-or half-day programming, definition of a "school year," and so on. Incredible as is may seem, little is known about the effects of different time arrangements on children in formal educational programs.

The third and final major category of curriculum model administrative policy explored here involves provisions for ongoing program evaluation: determining the worth of integral model components and, ultimately, the model as a whole. These provision can be classified into formative and summative evaluation tasks. Formative evaluation-instrumental during the early stages of model development and implementation-addresses the extent and quality of intended services. In contrast, summative evaluation address the overall worth of a model program at some terminal or critical decision point. Program administrators may also find it desirable even necessary in an increasingly economics- minded society-to apply principles of cost analysis to program evaluation. If so, summative model impact is studied in terms of cost efficiency, cost-benefit, cost utility, or cost effectiveness.

A cost-effectiveness approach will involve evaluation for the purpose of gaining maximum results for the lowest or most reasonable expenditure. Both formative and summative evaluation procedures demand careful attention to the selection of appropriate measurement and data-analysis techniques. Also important for this aspect of administrative policy are personnel qualification's authority, and responsibilities for evaluation. Generally speaking, insiders familiar with the workings of model have both an advantage and a vested interest in "trouble-shooting" their program and providing constructive feedback to other staff for program improvement. In contrast, qualified and disinterested external evaluation specialists are usually better situated to provide objective summative evaluation. In either case, administrative guidelines to justify the role definition and selection of evaluation personnel are at issue.

Administrative policies comprise a major category of curriculum model characteristics. These policies encompass practical decision making about personnel, physical facilities, and program evaluation. Ideally, policies are consistent with, if not determined directly by, overall model philosophy. Any set of model administration policies must be accompanied by a master fiscal policy, usually to include cost-accounting procedures. Fiscal concerns will be model-specific though general principles for budgeting and accounting can apply. Interested readers may consult Candoli et al. for further information. The joint issues of what and how best to educate young children have persisted unabated since the earliest days of formal educational thought. Neither issue is easily divorced from model philosophy and aims nor conveniently isolated from administrative policy decisions. For present purposes, however, content concerns the *what* of learning and its general arrangement in a curriculum: methods concerns presentation strategies-the *how* of curriculum delivery. Generally speaking, model philosophy and content selection go hand in hand. For example, a model based upon a philosophy of essentialism will be defined in content by a selected body of knowledge to which all children are exposed, ecological variables notwithstanding. Key issues associated with this philosophical stance include justifying the essentials and determining valid means or securing their achievement. Fixed or uniform levels of mastery or minimum competence for children in advance of instruction are compatible with this position. Content selection for a second model, in contrast, may spring from a moral imperative. This means that, to whatever extent possible, children should have freedom to exercise their own learning styles, choose their own content, and determine their own competence standards. Given this imperative, neither uniform content nor fixed ideas about pedagogy figure strongly in educational planning, Somewhere in between essentialism and the moral imperative for self-determined education may emerge a moderate, child-centered position to emphasize opportunity for content choices from among a varied but limited set of options. Emphases vary even among moderate positions. One long-standing content distinction in early education concerns learning for cognitive- intellectual achievement on the one hand and affective-social growth on the other. Cognitive-affective distinctions, of course, can easily strike a false or artificial dichotomy when, in truth, such leanings are highly interrelated.

Yet, the distinction is important, especially for scrutiny of content priorities within a curriculum model. It is instructive to not that educational applications of integrated cognitive and social development theory have been proposed.

A second, related distinction for curriculum model analysis is academic skills or subject matter proficiency versus intellectual content or cognitive skills proficiency. A primarily academic emphasis concerns acquisition of predetermined factual material along traditional subject mater lines. Intellectual content, however, is concentrated more upon the heuristic of learning; general inquiry skills, elaboration skills, and problems-solving strategies. Theoretically, a cognitive - intellectual skills approach is independent from academic content. If so, academic content is seen as a means to an end, not as an end in itself.

It seems fair to say that uncertainty, if not confusion and wariness, pervades decision making about content for early childhood education. Research has not yet confirmed much about what program contents are best for successive levels of early education. Promising rationales for content selection have been proposed, but they are infrequently applied in practice. Perhaps the most basic content issue for educators to address concerns a functional taxonomy for classifying educational content and objectives. To date, standard, consensual taxonomy permeates early childhood educational model building; nor is consensus likely in view of theoretical foundation differences among models.

A constructivist approach, for example, may use the Piagetian categories of physical, social, and logical knowledge. Curriculum models for intellectually precocious children are frequently governed by Guliford's structure of intellect theory to emphasize figural, symbolic, semantic, and behavioral content, Still other taxonomies are used for educational planning and evaluation despite nagging questions about their empirical validity. The taxonomy issue prompts a further specification of three integral content components important for the conceptual analysis of curriculum models: scope, priorities, and structure. Scope refers to the breadth or variety of content and skill values built into a curriculum model. One model may incorporate content across a broad spectrum, such as *aesthetics, cognitive intellectual skills, basic concept acquisition academics,* and *social-affective* skills. Other models may emphasize fewer skills domains, even to exclude certain content areas such as academics or aesthetics. Closely related to scope are the relative priorities assigned to content within a curriculum model. One clear indicator of priorities is amount of time allocated for content exposure. The variable *time of exposure* is critical for estimating children's opportunities for both acquisition and rehearsal or practice as well as practicing learnings. Exposure time can be operationalized in various ways, as, for example, by "time on task" or sheer duration of learning events. Either way, important links to curriculum methods surface here, especially pacing and intensity of stimulation.

Multiple interactions between and among content and methods variables can thus be proposed for empirical study. Such interactions are particularly notable in the brouhaha surrounding basic language training and remediation for young children. A third major content component variable is content *organization* or *structure* with accompanying rationales about sequencing content for different modes of instruction. Again, theoretical foundations are at least implicit in prescriptions for structuring content. One model, for example, may reflect armchair analysis of the structure of knowledge. Another may draw upon experimental task analysis procedures. Still another may base content organization and structure upon broad developmental sequences of cognition, as disclosed by longitudinal and cross-sectional research with children. However, it may be conceptualized, content structure provides another continuum insofar as analysis is concerned. At one extreme of this continuum are tightly organised, immutable content sequences prescribed for all children. At the other extreme are content structures supported by the moral imperative. These latter structures may be arbitrarily determined or conceivably, based upon comprehensive assessment of individual readiness for learning.

There is some degree of consensus among theoreticians that much of human learning and development is hierarchical in nature. Consensus is lacking, however, about the precise nature of hierarchical learning and the conditions or forces that influence hierarchical progression. A issue is a basis for structuring educational content over time for most effective learning, retention, and transfer. Controversy along these lines seems most pointed in the extent to which model advocates believe that *external* organization if content and general learning activities is desirable or necessary for given learning outcomes. Some additional content variables relevant to this discussion are *continuity* and *stability* or *regularity* in curriculum experience.

To the extent that thematic content is introduced, built upon, sustained, and integrated during a given instructional day, one can speak of continuity. To illustrate, consider a teacher who introduces selected grammatical structures during formal language training and then integrates these same structures with other lessons later in the day, such as musical songs, poetry, and arithmetic story problems. A common learning can thus be reinforced while simultaneously providing the occasion for generalization or transfer of learning. Stability refers to the extent to which a particular pattern of curriculum encounters recurs with predictable regularity, as daily, weekly, and so on. Model content high in stability will be revealed by specific curriculum routines. A model may prescribe that each day open with a group planning activity and close with a group evaluation of things accomplished. The interim period would be filled with an established order of content-related activities. Presumably, stability is important for children as an aid to time perspective development, sequential thinking, and general emotional security. If so, curriculum stability may be more or less important, depending upon age and expe iential background of the children involved. But a compulsive regularity, with few breaks from routine, conceivably could result in boredom and fatigue among some children. By the same token, insufficient regularity could breed anxiety and frustration among others. These ideas are relatively unested but appear together with other related hypotheses about the psychology of the open classroom. A final content variable is how content and skills emphases are translated into program objectives.

One feature of curriculum objectives readily culled from model analysis is the extent to which objective are explicit and operationalized for appropriate assessment. In general, model objectives most suited to reliable measurement are specific, precise, and stated in terms of observable behavior. The objective will state what a learner should be able to do, under what level of competency. A rich literature on the characteristics and application of behavioral objectives has accumulated together with many attendant issues about their utility and effects. Some content domains have been more amenable to behavioral phraseology than others. Consequently, models may present varying degrees of specificity and precision across content domains. Models are far from uniform in their affinity for behavioral objectives and choice of measurement strategy. At the theoretical level, any set of content or skill objectives, however, operationalized, should flow consistently form the overall goals or global, long-rang aims are revealed in curriculum philosophy. Unfortunately, rationales for translating broad, general program goals into specific objectives for instructional design are obscure, if extant, in many contemporary models.

The clarity, relevance, and appropriateness of curriculum content objectives surface as basic criteria for decisions about pupil progress assessment and model program evaluation. Still larger educational issues surface as well, including program accountability functions, how a curriculum model for young children may fit into broader developmental perspective, and measure-ment philosophy. As with curriculum content, methods are conceptualised described in many different ways. Standard designations of general methods come immediately to mind-tutorial, discussion, recitation, lecture, laboratory demonstrations- each of which has its own strengths and limitations insofar as establishing conditions for learning is concerned. More basic for conceptual analysis, however, is a set of methodological dimensions or processes that can be described as didactic versus prepared and group versus individual. A didactic versus prepared methods dimension concerns the extent to which teachers engage in expository teaching in contrast to more indirect means for preparing or arranging the learning environment to facilitate children's active involvement and self-initiated discovery learning. At issue are the how's and why's of alternative teacher-learner role enactment, that is, role definition in relation to curriculum objectives. Likewise, the group versus individual dimension involves a relative preference for group-based activities common for all learners or the desires of individualized learning experiences. Group-based activity unusually emphasizes uniform presentation and teacher-controlled recitation strategies. Although group may range in size, adult- child interactions typically dominate with varying degrees of freedom for child-child interactions. Programs that emphasize individualized experiences can also present a wide range of adult-child interactions with considerable attention to tutorial relationships, self-pacing, varied-child materials, and ample peer interactions. In practice, model programs rarely show an exclusive preference for one or the other methodological format. Dominant patterns of experience are common, however, and different combinations of methods may very through time. Thus, there are model differences in *;pacing,* wherein the frequency and rapidity of alternative individual-group and prepared-didactic experiences are salient concerns. Decisions about pacing various combinations of experience imply beliefs about what means are more or less suitable for what ends. For example, small-group activities my be preferred to promote children's cooperative behaviour; individualized discovery methods may be introduced to promote autonomous problem solving; and so on. Such beliefs or preferences about means -end relations provide a rich source of research hypotheses-for field research.

However basic the covering dimensions of didactic-prepared and group-individual methods are, additional variables further illustrate the methods substructure of curriculum models. For example, *formal assessment strategies* to determine children's program entry behaviour usually figure prominently in any diagnostic-prescriptive instructional; design, regardless of whether the learning task in question are introduced at a group or at an individual level. *Motivational strategies* also come into play. Curriculum models frequently differ in their emphasis upon activating and nurturing intrinsic motives or incentive systems that constitute extrinsic sources of motivation. The issue of relations between intrinsic motivation and extrinsic rewards has intensified in recent years, partly because of strong behavioristic influences in early childhood education. Current research issues, by no means resolves, include the study of learn of learning's sake. A related motivational strategy variable under study is classroom goal structure: the relative emphasis placed upon cooperative and competitive activity as he antecedent to group versus individual rewards and recognition, respectively. A methods dimension closely tied with motivation psychology is the preferred style of teacher-child interaction to include corrective feedback strategies, Some research issues here are teacher's question-asking strategies and their effects, how best to deal with the wrong response, the role of different types and schedules of reinforcement for different kinds of learning, and nonverbal communications in teaching.

A second class of human interaction variables in model development concerns peer tutorial methods and cooperative team learning strategies. This class of variables reflects a growing research interest in the *Learning Through Teaching* movement. Recent methods and results of various peer-tutoring and group-investigation strategies are reviewed by Sharan.

Still another class of instructional methods important for model analysis includes procedures for facilitating retention and positive transfer of learning. As for enhancing retention, especially long-term effectiveness of learning, several instructional design variables are noteworthy: procedures for generating meaning-fulness of children's new learning, assisting children it develop coding strategies for effective memory storage and retrieval, and appropriate practice and review tactics. In turn, securely retrained learnings are a necessary, though insufficient, condition for positive transfer. By this is meant the extent to which school learnings facilitate later performance and learning, both in and out of the school context.

It is tempting to argue that transfer is what school is all about. Theoretically, models designed to prepare children for successful adaptation to future schooling should show a strong commitment to vertical transfer; early, simpler learnings are purported to facilitate learning of later, more complex, and subordinate learnings. Models that stress acquisition of problem-solving strategies or "learning how to learn" imply a bias for skills that serve children well in an unpredictable and changing world. In any case, methods to promote transfer will have in common a focus on rules or principles that have broad generality, varied application of these rules and principles that have broad generality, varied application of these rules and principles, explicit procedures to establish a set to transfer, and soon. A problem for model analysis is the extent to which a formal theory of transfer guides the process of instructional design. A final method component to be discussed here is the orchestration of instructional media and materials: how sensory equipment, audio-visual resources, simulation games, autotelic devices, kits, workbooks, and other resources are coordinated and used. Variety in instructional media and materials is basic to any system of individualised instruction and enables a flowing of stimulation across different sensory modalities to maintain children's attention and reinforce learning. Appropriately scheduled, then novelty effect of various media theoretically can also sustain motivation for learning. It is important, of course, to distinguish among the mere presence of alternative media sources, their quality, how these sources are used, and their effects on educational development. Much has been learned about the impact of instructional media variables on learning that is useful to model builders. But with the possible exception of television studies, media research with preschool children seems to have lagged behind that with older learners.

Given young children's natural propensity for play, there seems to be a strong potential for games approaches to learning. These include physical activities to reinforce academic skills and group games for coordinated human development. Research possibilities seem especially promising for the media component of early childhood curriculum models. The curriculum methods dimension of curriculum models can be defined in terms if certain basic criteria. These criteria include the didactic-prepared, individual-group distinction as well as preassessment strategies, motivational procedures, interaction style, feedback procedures, provisions for transfer, and instructional resources. Choice of instructional methods is tied directly to beliefs about the conditions of learning. That is, methods comprise means to manipulate the ways in which children receive, price's, and act upon information from the environment. Thus, any set of prescribed methods presumably will reflect hypotheses about what conditions are essential for learning efficiency and effectiveness. In short, a theory of instruction is at issue. These collective ideas may be more or less well-founded in the empirical studies about children's learning. This foundation itself is an important point for scrutiny in model analysis; and a scrutiny of the methods component brings us back full cycle to the theoretical foundations component as a basis for decision making in model implementation.

Discerning readers may have noted that, excepting a brief reference to interaction style, nothing explicit has been written about the general social-affective climate for learning as a model component. Few would challenge the importance of this variable, however elusive its operationalization. Certainly the variable has a long-standing educational research interest as indicated by the literature on teacher, teaching style. From humanistic perspectives, education rhetoric supports the value of a warmly responsive, benevolent learning environment as best for young children. Humanists may call for the nurturant emotional climate primarily on moral grounds; but empirical data, such as a negative relationship between teacher's use of hostile criticism and children's achievement and attitudes towards school are also germane to this point.

However passionate any rhetoric, the research issue here is how well an intended emotional climate occurs in model implementation. Both administrative and instructional personnel are key factors in this aspect of implementation. Children themselves also contribute to classroom climate in several ways, the attitudes and expectancies they bring initially to the formal setting their reinforcement that occurs in the classroom, and so on. In larger perspective, though curriculum models may be analyzed on conceptual grounds independent of any social context, their implementation and effectiveness cannot. And both the implementation and the impact of a given model may vary with the context in which implementation occurs. Eventually, then, the validity of a model must be determined from the observation of real events. This prompts a shift from the conceptual blueprint stage of model analysis to issues and procedures of model implementations and impact evaluation research.

The basic technical thrust for curriculum model evaluation is determining how, when, and from what sources information will be gathered and analyzed for decision-making purposes. Thus, evaluation contributes to decisions, certification and installation. Accordingly, a systematic approach to model evaluation will begin by clarifying the purpose of evaluation. Once the purpose is clarified, problem solving about suitable evaluation methodology follows. Decisions about model program development and improvement, for example, call for the application of formative evaluation procedures. Decisions about program continuation or adoption will call for evidence of program impact or total effectiveness. Hence, summative evaluation procedures are necessary. Both kinds of procedures may be combined to promote understanding of basic psychological or social processes, depending upon the extent to which this kind of information is central to the evaluation effort. A specification of procedures for both formative and summative evaluation, or model implementation and impact evaluation, will comprise an evaluation design. The main components of an evaluation design are the conditions, schedule, and type if data collection and analysis, details of which are discussed elsewhere. Model impact or outcome evaluation has been dominated by applications of experimental; and quasi-experimental research methods. Although the feasibility of such methods is usually limited in field settings, these methods have earned an important place in educational evaluation. The literature on formative evaluation procedures is less extensive, but nonetheless important for students of curriculum models. Moreover, conceptual systems for determining the adequacy of comprehensive evaluation designs are noteworthy for study. Traditionally, decision making about early childhood model evaluation has been dominated by summative or outcome evaluation research especially to seek immediate, short-term evidence of model impact on children. The merit of curriculum models typically has been assessed according to how clearly models produce desired or intended changes among children exposed to them. Support or opposition to a model then, is rallied on the basis of evidence about children's progress in academic achievement and other valued goal areas.

However preoccupied evaluators have been with summative impact evaluation, a meaningful empirical test of any model clearly requires that certain basic assumptions be met. A first is that stated outcomes are attainable through educational processes. This calls forth again the rationale by which realistic and worthwhile goals and objectives are selected, formulated, judged, and linked to instructional design. A second requisite assumption for meaningful model impact evaluation is that valid, reliable measures are available to assess goal achievements. The assumption of technically respectable measurement has been difficult to meet fully in practice. Satisfactory assessment of young children's educational progress poses peculiar challenges to evaluation. Not only have measurement strategies been limited in scope and technique, but evaluators have also tended to place ease of measurement above quality control. Evaluation has been heavily dependent upon the use of spurious testing procedures. Such problems and challenges to evaluation are discussed elsewhere as are the matters of measurement availability, construction, selection, and evaluation. Few will deny, however, that model impact data are only as valid as the procedures used to gather however, that model impact data are only as valid as the procedures used to gather them. Associated issues for model outcome evaluation are determining what effects are worth assessing and how they shall be assessed. The third assumption for meaningful model impact evaluation is that a model is, in fact, implemented as prescribed or intended. The importance of this condition cannot be overemphasized.

A given model can easily be jeopardized on grounds of "no effects" or "poor results" in the absence of data about how adequately, completely, or competently it was implemented. The alleged early failure of Project Head Start illustrates this problem. That is, data from a limited range of generic, short-range measurements were taken virtually at face value to judge the effectiveness of compensatory intervention before any semblance of implementation quality could be determined. Premature and narrowly conceived evaluation seriously threatened Head Start's existence; and controversy about Head Start models impact has continued to persist still short of adequate implementation data.

The Head Start object lesson among others, has contributed to a greater appreciation of process evaluation: assessing the merit of program variables antecedent to and presumably related in a causal way to program outcomes. Process variables encompass curriculum methods and materials, teacher personality or style, emotional climate, and characteristics of the physical environment. In conventional experimental research parlance, process variables collectively constitute the "treatment," that is, the independent variable(s) to which subjects are exposed and upon which predictions about change are based. Process evaluation, then is, concerned with the problem of insuring that the treatment has occurred.

The importance of this insurance for valid impact evaluation has already been stressed. But process evaluation is more and more valued for its own sake. For one thing, overall program quality is at issue. For another, process valuation is well suited to questions about what instructional methods and materials are best tailored to or most preferred by given program personnel. For still another, explicit process-outcome linkages are probably best understood through the careful examination and systematic manipulation of treatment variables.

Process approaches to curriculum model evaluation depend heavily upon, but are not limited to, observational techniques. Consequently, a basic problem or process evaluation is selecting or developing an appropriate system for taking and recording observational data. Child development and early education researchers have provided a wealth of observational systems and procedures, many of which are aptly illustrated by curriculum model implementation and impact studies. Interview and questionnaire methods figure prominently in innovative approaches to determine the level of program implementation in specific educational settings. Systematic process evaluation procedures for measuring domains of instruction have also been proposed, the most detailed of which concern variations on the theme of mastery learning and prescriptive teaching. Arguments for integrating ethnographic techniques in the model research and evaluation activity have appeared with increasing frequency during the past several years as well. For evaluators who fear that use of such techniques undermines objectivity in evaluation research, strategies for dealing with the issue of subjectivity can be recommended.

Further developments in early education evaluation

As progress in process evaluation continues, so does thinking about how to broaden the scope of impact evaluation for a better understanding of educational processes. One practice championed for this purpose is the multivariate analysis of model programs. Conventional evaluation practice has usually been limited to documenting average gains for groups of children involved in one or another model program. Multivariate analysis seeks to disclose interactions between child and program characteristics, that is, to determine which program characteristics are more or less important in accounting for variations in children's responses to programs.

This sort of analysis has been slow ın application to routine evaluation methodology bit it figures prominently for questions about why some children may flourish in a given program while other may not. The more basic line of scholarly inquiry involved here, of course, is the increasingly popular aptitude-or trait-treatment interaction research. Practical applications of this form of inquiry are they uncertain. Conceptually, however, this inquiry seems pertinent to solving problems about matching children to treatment, that is, finding the "best fit" between programs and their participants. A second, related idea for improved curriculum model evaluation concerns adaptations of longitudinal research methodology to better monitor long-term program effects on children, parents, and staff. Much of the impetus for this "cumulative impact" approach to evaluation emanates from exemplary programs, as the Perry Preschool Project, and the consortium for longitudinal studies. The push for standard longitudinal evaluation is, in part, a reaction to swarms of skeptics who question the values of early education.

Broadly conceived longitudinal evaluation seems now recognized as essential for a more complete understanding of education and development. Fundamental questions concerning type of intervention programs, duration and intensity of intervention, and amount of family involvement can all be dealt with at a more sophisticated level through longitudinal evaluation. Some authorities advocate that evaluation should be planned and conducted from a truly developmental perspective. Though cumulative, long-term impact is important from this perspective, more critical for ongoing evaluation are program quality a participant response to it. Qualitative change among both children and staff, especially in terms of realizing human potentials, becomes more central to evaluation than the conventional behavioural assessment of child outcomes. Still other authorities call for fundamental reformation in evaluation practice. Among other things, reformation would require a softening of demands for technical purity in evaluation and greater commitment to progressive enlightenment, that is, a more complete understanding of program operations within their sociopolitical contexts. Relevance and credibility, not scientific quality, become principal standards from which evaluations are planned, executed, analyzed, and disseminated. Broadened perspectives on evaluation can often be clarified or enhanced by reference to one or another *conceptual framework* from which to chart essential evaluation tasks.

Thus, conceptual frameworks are available for planning formative-summative procedures, determining accountability to clientele, identifying deficiencies in staff training, determining the effectiveness of innovative programs and assessment, evaluating the context in which a model program may be implemented, evaluating unintended or unanticipated model outcomes, and other purposes. Such frameworks, usually called evaluation models, show still another use of the term "model." Use of an evaluation model appropriate to the various purposes of curriculum model evaluation is inherently sensible for any systematic, logical, and consistent approach to decision making about the worth of program process and outcomes. Among the more sensitive areas of decision making applied to early education is economics. Economic theory holds that continual investment in a given enterprise or opportunity is warranted insofar as that enterprise or opportunity shows or continues to yields "better returns" than alternatives would. In the context of early education, this theory guides a variety of cost-analysis procedures that concern measuring costs in relation to program effectiveness, efficiency, benefits to participants, and so on. Methodological problems abound in this approach to evaluation; but impressive instances of cost analysis can be cited to indicate that the expense incurred by competently implemented model program may be compensated by long-term benefits to society. Interested readers should consult the technical literature for details. A final issue for curriculum model evaluation concerns the external validity of a model program, or the power of a model to produce similar effects across a wide variety of specific settings. Models are implemented in particular environmental contexts.

Evaluation proceeds to validate their implementation, goal achievements, and even cost efficiency of effectiveness. But this documentation is insufficient to conclude that a given curriculum model will be equally effective under different environmental conditions and with different populations of consumers. There is a need for replicative evaluation research to better understand any intersite variation in model processes and outcomes. Needs, resources, personnel competencies, and support services are but a few potentially significant factors in intersite variation. The Project follow Through evaluation is a ample precedent for showing that the same model may "work" better in some contexts than in others, even when instructional procedures are comparable across sites. Since much remains to be learned about such variation, caution against any premature generalization of model effects is advised. Models, even when refined to the point of high exportability, seem subject to subtle social forces. It appears that staff commitment to a model and the extent to which the values of a particular community are met through that model are among the most critical of these forces. Comprehensive curriculum model evaluation will include both process and impact assessment in a longitudinal perspective with an eye toward reconciling cost with benefits to individuals and the larger society. Considerably progress has been made in the methodology for this purpose, a study of which is a requisite for genuine professionalism in early childhood education. A curriculum model is an ideal conceptual structure for decision making about educational aims, administrative policies, curriculum content, and instructional methods. Educational philosophy and psychological theory combine to form the core of a comprehensive curriculum model. From those core are generated policy guidelines for the selection of curriculum goals and objectives. Goals and objectives normally indicate degrees of emphasis upon education for cultural competence, naturalistic growth, and preparation for the future. At issue is a rationale or justification for taking any value stance about the functions of organized education for young children. Internally consistent administrative policies are also governed by theory in a thoroughly formulated curriculum model. Administrative policies have been classified into three interrelated categories. A first category-personnel specification-involves criteria for the target population of learners, program staff, and community involvement. Considerations about the physical setting or curriculum model development comprise a second category of administrative policy. The third is program evaluation policy. This category calls for decisions about formative-summative evaluation and may be juxtaposed with cost-accounting procedures.

Curriculum content and method were discussed in terms of distinctions among academic skills, cognitive-intellectual development, and effective growth. The issue of a functional taxonomy for defining content emphasis was highlighted along with decision points about content priorities and the organization of content sequences. Arrangements for continuity-stability in content delivery and the issue of operational statements of curriculum model objectives were also discussed. Method variables in curriculum modes were examined in relation to two interlocking dimensions: didactic versus prepared, and group versus individual methods. Implications of these choices were framed against strategies, procedures for securing retention and transfer of learning, and the use of instructional media and materials. Content-method issues were couched more broadly in the trend to study early education from an ecological perspective.

Examining curriculum models form the standpoint of formal evaluation involves a series of decisions about evaluation purpose(s), design and analysis, and the application of results. Evaluation or level or fidelity of implementation was distinguished from evaluation for cumulative model impact. Needs and trends in model evaluation research were also reviewed. These include more sophisticated process evaluation to establish process-outcome linkages, the longitudinal-multi-variate analysis of model impact, cost-utility applications, and the quest to establish external validity for innovative models.

7

Language in Young Children

Perhaps nothing has been discussed and debated as frequently or as fervently in educational circles as the topic of how children come to comprehend and create written language, that is, how they learn to read and write. The time and space devoted to this topic indicate its importance in the goal structure of our schools and society as well as its failure to yield to simple problems into its mysteries. Much research in the area of reading has investigated the effects of various instructional methods used in beginning reading: the language experience approach versus phonics, linguistic readers versus basals, the initial teaching alphabet versus the standard alphabet, and so on. These investigation, however, have yielded little information about the best way to teach children to read: "Regardless of the quantity of research...there are no definitive answers to the question of the best program because the results of various studies support different programs, and nothing conclusive can be shown about which programs are superior"

It should be acknowledged, however, that several large studies, in which many individual studies of instructional methods have been surveyed or in which their results have been analyzed as a group, have found small but significant differences in favor of methods emphasizing some kind of systematic phonies instruction. A recent study of this type also found the sound-symbol method to be superior over other methods. In addition, however, the study found that experimental treatments regardless of method produced higher achievement than control methods. The researchers urged caution about their results.

The significant effect found for sound-symbol methods could have been "due to chance in the testing of many effects". Others have pointed out that competing explanations were not adequately discounted and that the results could have been due to higher learning time for students in some programs, unusual teacher characteristics, a better match between teaching and testing in experimental programs, and differences in pace and task selection. It appears, then, that this line of inquiry is beset with problems and yields conflicting results. Because the question of which method is best has generally proved to be an unproductive one, this review will not provide any discussion of research specifically aimed at comparing instructional methods used in beginning reading. Instead, I will concentrate on research and clinical observations that have attempted to understand reading in terms of basic psychological and linguistic processes and/or have tried to determine what concepts about written language young children bring with them to formal reading instruction and what experiences contribute to their development.

It has often been assumed that children know little or nothing about written language before they receive formal instruction in school. Evidence indicates, however, that children do have extensive knowledge of some aspects of written language.

Many preschoolers have knowledge about the graphic features of print. They know that the features of lines used in print are different from lines used to make pictures or other nonprint configurations. The features contrasted in one study of three-to six-and-one-half-year-olds were pictures versus writing, linear versus nonlinear arrangement of units, internally varied versus repetitive sequences of units, and multiple units versus single units. Still other displays contained Roman or cursive letters and words, artificial letters, Hebrew letters, a Mayan design, and Chinese characters. Even the youngest children distinguished between pictures and writing, though they often labeled as writing nonpictorial displays that were not writing, basing judgments on gross features of the displays, such as linearity, variety of units, and multiplicity of units. The older children tended to base judgments on actual features of individual units within a display rather than on features of the total display. Thus, the more that units in the display resembled actual letters occurring in the child's environment the greats the tendency for the display to be labeled as writing, regardless of the display's general characteristics.

A similar developmental trend has been found in studies of preschool children's productions of writing. Two early studies found roughly four stages of development. First, scribbles became horizontal rather than aimless or basically circular. Then displays became linear and jagged, suggesting knowledge of both linearity and multiplicity of units as features of writing. In stage three, features of real letters, such as straight, curved, or intersecting lines, but no actual letters, were found. Stage four was characterized by the appearance of actual letters, or good approximations to these. In summary, development moved from representation of overall characteristics of print to representations of the distinctive features of letters. In a recent study, four-year-olds were instructed to "write everything you can write." Each child's scribble resembled the writing system to which the child had been exposed most frequently, even though no child's sample contained real units of print. Nejeeba, the child attempting to write Arabic, told the researcher that Arabic uses "a lot more dots than English". This research indicates that before children receive formal instruction in reading and writing, and often before they accurately name letters or recognize words, they abstract features of writing from the print they encounter from exposure to print provided in their everyday environments. Young children may, of course, differentiate among graphic displays, that is, determine visually some of its properties, but not understand how to use it or what purposes it serves. For example, children who can detect differences in pictorial and print displays and label one writing and not the other may point to pictures rather than print in a storybook when indicating what the reader looks at. In short, children may recognize print versus nonprint but know nothing of the reading process. Some research has indicated that young children know little about what a reader does or what the reading process entails. Two studies of five-year-olds, for example, demonstrated that many children did not know what adults do when they read or that words rather than pictures in books are what one reads. Research by Hiebert, however, suggests that many preschoolers may know more than earlier research has revealed. Early studies posed questions in abstract situations rather than in more concrete contextualized situations where children could show rather than tell what they know. In addition, the children studied previously may not have been provided opportunities to interact with print in their daily lives. In Hiebert's study, understanding of the reading process was measured by three tasks. In one, the researcher read silently and orally from a book and also stared silently at an object. Children were asked to name each activity performed by the researcher. The second task asked children to read a "secret message". This stimulus was used to ask children about their reading ability and to infer their understanding of the reading process if they attempted to "read" the page. The third task used several books: (1) one with pictures and text; (2) one with pictures only; (3) one with text only; and (4) one with bland pages. Children were asked if each book could be read by someone who could read and if yes, what such a reader would look at. These tasks were designed to reveal children's basic ideas about reading, such as whether reading requires speaking while looking at a book or can be done silently and whether print versus pictures are what one looks at to read.

Hiebert also investigated preschoolers' understanding of the functions of writing. Story situations were used. For example, children were shown Christmas packages and asked how one would know to which family member each package was to be given. Each package was tagged with a news label. If the child did not refer to this label, he or she was asked who it was for. Three stories used a model town complete with buildings street signs, road signs, and toy cars. One of these presented two cars approaching an intersection. Children were asked how the drivers would know what to do to avoid a crash. A fifth story used materials and directions for a children's game.

The experimenter explained that children wanted to play this new game but did not know how. Was there a way they could find out? Between three and five years of age, children's concepts about reading processes and functions increase significantly, and in this middle class sample greater gains occurred between three and four than between four and five. These changes apparently occurred as a result of informal encounters with print in the course of everyday events. While all sixty subjects were enrolled in a nursery school or day-care center, neither offered any formal reading instruction.

Additional evidence that preschool children develop knowledge about reading processes or about what one does while reading comes from studies of children's story-reading behavior. Doake and Rossman, for example, found that the preschool children they studied increased their awareness over time that readers look at the text when they read, and that reading involves looking at print in a book, not just saying words of a story that you know while looking at the pictures. Young children may know that one looks at words to read and that reading serves a variety of purposes, but not what characteristics distinguish a word from other segments of print, or how to determine if a print display shown to them is a word or something that does not quality as a word.

In a study by Pick at al, children were presented print displays on white cards. Word displays included single-letter words, long letter strings, short letter strings likely to be unfamiliar to the children, and fifteen five-letter words. Nonword displays included single letters; two long letter strings; ten four-letter consonant clusters; ten strings of misoriented letters, of which five could be words and five that could not; four groups of meaningful initials sounded like real words. Variables contrasted were length of a letter string, whether a string was an actual word, vowel and consonant strings only versus strings with both consonant and vowels, letter orientation, and meaning. The subjects were twenty-three- and four-year-old nursery school children, older by one-half year than the oldest nursery school children, seventeen kindergarten children, older by one-half year than the oldest nursery school children; sixteen first-grade children, and thirteen second and third grade children. Children were asked to sort the cards into those that had words and those that did not. Younger nursery school children were significantly more likely than older nursery school children to accept single letters as words, whether they wee words or not.

The preschool children also accepted a higher percentage of the very long letter strings as words. This tendency decreased with age, with the oldest children accepting very long strings only when these were real words. The percentage of vowel-only and consonant-only when these were real words. The percentage of vowel-only and consonant-only clusters accepted as words decreases with age, with significant differences occurring both between nursery school and kindergarten and kindergarten and first grade. Acceptance of strings containing declined significantly between the nursery and kindergarten groups and again between kindergarten and first grade groups. Acceptance of pronounceable non-kindergarten and between the nursery and kindergarten groups and again between kindergarten and first grade groups. Acceptance of pronounceable non-words that sounded like meaningful words decreased between nursery school ad kindergarten and between first and second grade but even the oldest children still accepted a large percentage of them as words.

Acceptance of pronounceable clusters that were not meaningful declined with age, with sharp declines between kindergarten and first grade and between first grade and second grade. These results indicate that before the beginning of formal instruction in reading, children begin to understand something about word structure. Between kindergarten and first grade when formal instruction has still been somewhat minimal, substantial gains are made.

The youngest children were more likely to classify both single letters and letter strings as words. But by five, children knew that words generally are composed of several letters and that letters and that letters and words are different entities. Older children also rejected very long strings, unless they were real words, indicating that they knew a word is not defined simply by a string of letters, but by internal characteristics of the string as well, such as the arrangement of the letters and whether when sounded out they result in a meaningful word. Similarly, by kindergarten age, children more and more rejected strings that were all vowels or all consonants, indicating again that they knew that wordness is determined by characteristics within the letter strings-that there are permissible strings and nonpermissible strings. A letter string by itself does not constitute wordness. Finally, as children got older, particularly between kindergarten and first grade, they rejected letter strings that were pronounceable but meaningless, as well as pronounceable nonwords that were meaningful, with the former showing the stronger decline. Apparently, as children get older they use their ability to sound out strings, as well as their knowledge of how words look, to judge wordness. If sounding out results in a meaningful word, they are likely to judge that the letter string is a word. Other studies and clinical observations have yielded similar results. When matching speech to print in storybooks, for example, the youngest and/or least experienced preschoolers often point to individual letters as if each were a word or syllable.

Forty the Snowman

Frosty the Snowman

Older or more experienced preschoolers more often attempt to read by responding to clusters of letters marked by space, although a word, as distinct from a syllable, in speech may still not be known to them.

Frosty the Snowman

Frosty the Snowman

Additional evidence comes from a second study by Hiebert in which children between three and four-and-one-half, shown cards in context and out of context, were asked. What might this say? Confusion between letters and words should have caused children to respond to single word displays with multiword responses. Yet, a high percentage of the responses for both in-context and out-of-context displays consisted of single words. Most children knew how to make correct printed word to spoken word correspondences, indicating that they knew, at minimum, that words consist of letter clusters-single letters are not words.

Even kindergarten and first grade children, however, cannot accurately determine what a printed word is when asked to respond to various print displays. Meltzer and Herse asked kindergarten and first grade children to use scissors to cut off words from printed sentences.

Children sometimes cut off one word, sometimes two, and sometimes only part of a word, indicating that they did not judge words in a line of print as clusters of letters set off from other clusters by space. The difference between the performance of these children and younger children who accurately point to individual printed words when reading storybooks could be due to their inability to monitor the print by using knowledge of what it said. In short, being able to detect individual words in print or in speech may be facilitated when the child knows what the print presented says. Getting the match between speech and print to come out right can serve as a monitor to judge what constitutes a word in both speech and print. Support for this hypothesis comes from a study of children just finishing the first month of school. Children were first taught a short poem orally. Then the researcher read the first line aloud and pointed along each word. Then the child was asked to finger-point and read the second, third, and fourth lines, which were framed with index cards. After each line was read, the examiner pronounced two target words within the line and asked the child to locate these. Next, the examiner and the child read the entire poem together twice as the examiner pointed to each word. The examiner then pointed to individual words within the poem and asked the child to pronounce them. Finally, the printed poem was taken away, and the child was asked to pronounce six words isolated from the text, one at a time. The four measures of word concepts were ability to: (1) point to words as one reads aloud: (2) recognise specific words within one line: (3) recognise specific words any where in the poem; and (4) recognize sight words. Although there was a wide range in success on these take, many children performed well, indicating that they could isolate words in both speech and print. Still other evidence of young children's understanding of word structure comes from their attempts to create words with manipulative alphabet materials or by writing rather than from their judgments about wordness in terms of displays of print presented to them. Research and clinical observations reveal that preschool children may at first string letters together at random to make words.

Such behaviour often occurs spontaneously as children play with alphabet materials. The child tells the adult that the creation is a "word" and even labels it, or the child may ask the adult." What does this word say?" At this stage, the child seems to know that words are composed of more than one unit, but not that such strings are organized in specific ways internally. Absent are visual criteria for permissible letter combinations, as well as any notion that the sequence of letters in a printed word must be related to the sequence of sounds in the spoken word. When the letter realizations dawns on children, they may give up visual criteria of wordness used earlier and rely on phonetic relationships when creating words even if knowledge of letter-sound relationships is limited to only one element of the word.

Henderson has designated a preliterate phonetic

stage of spelling in which dog is spelled D or DJ, and candy, K or KDE, by different children. What is common to all spellings for a given word at this stage is that letters selected to spell it must bear some phonetic relationship to the spoken word. What is different about various spellings is that at times children have used just one letter to spell the word, while at other times they have used more than one letter. It is impossible to know from Henderson's data if different children consistently used one strategy and not the other of if the same children used both strategies on different occasions. If they did not know how to represent more than one sound, they may have used only one letter rather than violate their knowledge that when making words, letters must be selected with this criterion in mind. Instead, they may have violated their knowledge that words consist of more than one letter.

Children lacking knowledge of phonetic relationships may use longer letter strings to make words because they judge wordness on the basis of characteristics they have obtained merely from seeing words; words are letter strings. Without phonetic constraints as a guide, stringing may get out of hand. In addition, if the child does not know that words in a line a print are surrounded by space, then exposure to printed text, as opposed to single words such as names or traffic signs, may lead them to believe that words can be very long. In addition, the number of letters used to make a particular word may be influenced by knowledge of the object whose name is spelled. Papandropoulou and Sinelair and Berthoud papandropoulou, for example, found that preschool children often justified a word's length in terms of characteristics of its referent, not in terms of the necessity to mach print to length of utterance. Crocodile is longer than cat because crocodiles are longer than cats. Typewriter is long because typewriters have lots of letters. Children who make judgments based on these criteria must know a little about the actual determinants of word structure, particularly that a printed word is related to its spoken counterpart. Apparently, knowing that a printed word is related to the spoken word in a specific way- that letters used to make a word must represent sounds in the spoken word-is a late development for many children. Henderson has suggested that the preliterate phonetic stage emerges by late kindergarten or beginning first grade. The second stage, called letter name strategy stage, emerges by mid-first grade. More complicated and sophisticated phonetic strategies appear by grade two and beyond. However, Read has reported preschool children as young as three-and one-half using phonetic strategies. Bissex, in a case study of her son, reports such behavior beginning at five.

The early emergence of phonetic strategies to create words in some preschool children seems to be related to the print-rich environments these children were reared in. The ingredients for precocious development seem clear: printed materials of various kinds; materials for creating print of one's own; adult mediation of print in the environment such as naming letters, writing the child's name, and modeling reading and writing; reading to children; answering the child's questions; and allowing the child wide latitude in exploring how words are created. Variations in documentation of children's knowledge of wordness appear to have two major sources: (1) variations in the populations studied; and (2) differences in definitions or aspects of wordness and methodologies used to study these. In summary, we can say only that some older preschool and kindergarten children seem to know something about what distinguishes words from nonwords, using both visual and meaning criteria, and that some older preschool and kindergarten children have general notions about criteria one must use to create words. But many children do not have such knowledge even upon entry into or completion of, first grade. They do not know a letter from a word or how words are constructed either by visual criteria or in relation to the spoken words they represent. Without it, they are likely to be confused by reading instruction. Speech may be represented in writing in a number of ways for example, at the word or syllable level. English orthography is based on representation of smaller segments; it is alphabetic. The linguistic unit represented by letters is the individual phoneme or sound. To use such a system, a reader must be able to segment and analyze oral language at the phonemic level. Researchers have tried to determine if young children can do this. The research indicates that analysis at the phonemic level is extremely difficult for the preschool and kindergarten age child.

Liberman et al, asked nursery, kindergarten, and first grade children to repeat a word or sound spoken by the researcher and to tap on the table with a dowel the number of segments contained in the stimulus item. Nursery school children could not segment stimuli into phonemes, although about half could segment words into syllables. About one fifth of the kindergarten children could segment by phonemes, while about half could segment by syllables. About 70 percent of the first graders could segment by phonemes, and 90 percent could segment by syllables.

Other researcher have also indicated that young children cannot analyze speech at the phonemic level and that this inability is related to difficulty in learning to read. Without the ability to segment at the phonemic level, that is, to hear three segments in bat, it would be difficult to know how speech is mapped on to an alphabetic orthography that provides one letter for each sound. The major difficulty in segmenting speech into phonemes seems to arise because there is no distinct acoustic segment which marks phonemes. "In bat, for example, the initial and final consonants are, in the conversion to sound, folded into the medial vowel, with the result that information about successive segments is transmitted more or less simultaneously on the same parts of the sound". Syllables, in contrast, are marked by a "peak of acoustic energy".

Our perception that words consist of distinct sounds is not as much a matter of perceptual reality as it is of conceptual development. We come to think or words in terms of individual sound segments, though they do not exist in "physical" reality. Although some children arrive at this basic insight before they receive formal reading instruction, most children develop it only before they receive formal reading instruction, most children develop it only after exposure to formal reading instruction. The insight escapes a few children even after considerable instruction, and many of these children have great difficulty in learning to read.

The absence of this insight is not due to faulty auditory or speech perception. A child who detects that the words bad and bat sound different, may not be able to segment each into three parts and say in which segment the difference occurs. The problem is centered more on becoming aware of analysis in speech at a level that is tied to printed letters; it involves knowing how to map speech to print. Conscious analysis at this level would not be necessary or useful if our orthography were not alphabetic. Experience with speech alone, even speech organized to highlight differences at the phoneme level, may not be enough. The idea of phonemes may not emerge in any concrete way unless the child is confronted with print and must find a use for all of the letters that make up the child's name or the words in a line of text in a favorite storybook. Print freezes the continuous stream of speech into perceptually manipulable blocks and begins to pull a child's tacit knowledge about words to the surface where an explicit understanding can being to develop.

Print appears to play a crucial but paradoxical role in turning the transparency of spoken language into the opaqueness of an object that can be studied-paradoxical because print is supposed to be a second order abstraction from reality, with spoken language being a first order abstraction. Logically, it would appear that print would be more difficult to grasp conceptually than spoken language. If we assume that to understand print entails a fairly elaborate explanation of its characteristics and function, then print may indeed be more difficult. If on the other hand we admit the virtues of tacit knowledge, then we see where print, by being a common and fairly stable symbolic system in the environment, draws the young child's attention to ward the abstract symbolic structure of language.

The same monitoring of speech used to find word segments corresponding to each letter cluster marked by space when following along a know story or poem text could lead ultimately to monitoring of speech to find segments that correspond to each letter within the cluster making a word. Solving this puzzle, or realising that it is a puzzle needing a solution, would seem to lead a child to the needed discovery. In Morris's study, there was a significant correlation between locating individual words in a poem known orally and performing successfully on a phoneme segmentation test. Knowing what words in print are and locating them were related to the ability to segment speech into phonemes. We can only speculate that being able to match words in speech to words in prints is a necessary step in the development of the ability to segment speech into phonemes and match these to letters within a word.

Oral knowledge of the text may be able to force changes in our understandings about print, and understandings of print may be able to force changes in understandings about language. This review would be incomplete without a brief discussion of children who learn to read before they begin formal instruction. Reports of these children have been provided by Durkin, plessas and Oakes, Sutton, Krippner, Torrey, Forester, Doake, and Witty and Coomer. For the most part, parents of such children did not set out to teach their children to read. In virtually all cases, however, children have come from print-rich environments. Being read to frequently was an experience common to almost all of these children. In addition, environmental print was interpreted by parents and read to the children. These children were also given materials such as paper and pencils or crayons, chalkboards, and manipulative alphabet materials. Finally, their parents responded to questions and requests. Parents also read the same stories over and over, pointed out words when the child asked. "Where does it say-?," provided appropriated demonstrations when children asked, for example, "How does an 'e' go?", and provided the letter when asked "How do you spell-?" While not setting out to teach children to read and not doing so in a formal way, the parents, nevertheless, provided essential experiences. It is difficult to translate research finding into suggestions for practice. Most of the research tells us what children can and cannot do, but little about what determines these abilities. In addition, we know little about how some of these concepts and abilities are related to each other or what other concepts and abilities, as yet unknown, are also critical. Despite these limitations, some tentative decisions can be made about practices that may be promising, and related issues can be considered. Because some preschool and kindergarten children have considerable knowledge about written language before receiving formal instruction, some researchers have claimed that learning to read is "natural," as natural as learning to speak. Other claim that learning to read is not "natural" because most children become readers only after specific tutoring. Learning to speak is natural, but learning to read is different, they claim. Perhaps both views are incorrect; perhaps learning to read is not different from learning to speak, and perhaps neither occurs "naturally"

The frequency with which a behavior occurs does not necessarily indicate anything about the basis for its development. We cannot assume, simply because oral language acquisition is almost universal, that it is innate or "natural," developing without environmental supports, or even instruction of a sort. Assuming that environmental supports for languages are virtually universal-robust and redundant-the universality of languages acquisition may depend not only on characteristics of the child but also on the environment. Because these characteristics have become commonplace, we fail to recognize their contribution and believe that language acquisition is "natural."

In formal development when control of the trunk is achieved in stable sitting posture, there is a smooth transition to bridging and creeping. In our sample, most of our babies achieved stability in sitting well within the range of sighted babies. Most of our babies demonstrated the ability to support themselves on hands and knees within the range for sighted babies. Then, something that should appear on the developmental timetable did not appear. The baby did not creep.

Since locating and reaching a toy on sound cues are the only ways in which the blind child can find equivalence for reaching and attaining an object on sight, there was no motive for reach. The sighted child, in the same posture, will reach for the out-of-reach toy which propels him forward. It is the visual incentive that initiates the creeping pattern...

At every point where vision would normally intervene to promote a new phase in locomotor development we had to help the baby find an adaptive solution. The prone position, for example, is not an "interesting" position for the blind baby. The sighted baby spends long in prone, with head elevated, "just looking around." The blind baby, without such incentives, may resist the prone position. We build in "interest" in prone through speaking to the baby, through dangle toys or other devices.....

Practicing pulling to stand and cruising will be "more interesting" in the familiar space of a playpen with favorite toys offering sound-touch incentives. Even motor development, typically thought to be controlled by genetic or maturational factors, is dependent on objects and people that are approached with the guidance of vision in sighted children. These supports are so abundant in most children's environments that it takes a study of visually impaired children to make us aware of their role. Extensive research has recently been conducted on the effects of adult language on infant language development. Adult linguistic input is often extensive, and the quality of the adult language influences the infant's language development.

Evidence that written language acquisition occurs without formal instruction only when appropriate social and physical environments are provided comes from almost every study of children who have learned read before they received formal instruction in school. Most of these children had extensive experience with print and tools for creating it, as well as interactions with parents who answered their children's questions, modeled reading, and read to them frequency. The fact that parents did not set out to teach their children to read and to write, and were often not aware that they were doing so, does not mean that they did not provide crucial experiences and supports. The evidence suggests that they did.

The term "natural" is not very useful. We might be wiser to think of the "given" characteristics of children as "invariant functions," to borrow an idea and terminology from Piaget. What is "given" are modes of adaptation or particular orientations to circumstances. The structure of intelligence, or what we come to know, is created or constructed through interactions between the child and the environment. Knowledge construction in a particular domain depends on access to experiences out of which that kind of knowledge can be created. Without such access, a "natural" learner cannot come to know.

All environments, no matter how commonplace, are contrived—they could be different. Experiences relating to some kinds of knowledge such as number. Space, and classification are so redundant, however, that universal acquisition of concepts could occur without adults being aware that they and the physical environment have made a contribution. The same may be said for oral language, but with a difference: a strong social environment would also be required. We need who read to them or respond positively to their questions, and no pencils or crayons and paper on which to attempt to write. The current disparities in the occurrence of oral and written language in the population may be due to disparities in the universal availability of environments that support each.

If written language acquisition in the way suggested, then we must do more than wait for it to emerge "naturally." We probably need not employ the "formal" instructional programs currently used in many primary grade classrooms. But "informal approaches" to reading instruction cannot be devoid of contact with print in context. Exposure to print experiences-actually, involvement in print experiences-can be incidental, but not accidental. Environments that are robust and redundant with print experiences must be deliberately contrived.

We must adopt the processes as well as the

content of effective parental practices. The practice of reading stories to young children, for example, often distorts and makes ineffective the parental reading situation. Parents read to individual children or to two or three who are in their lap or sitting close: Teachers read to groups of children sitting at a distance. Parents allow children to select the book to be read and reread the same book over and over again, both at the same sitting and over a period of weeks or months; teachers often select the book that is to be read and read it once at each sitting and infrequently in the course of a week or month. Parents allow children to turn the pages, pause to look at pictures or to ask questions, and read along if they wish. Teachers, on the other hand, are more likely to set the pace, turn the pages, and discourage reading along during the story episode. Parents keep their children's books accessible over a number of years: teachers often keep books out of children's reach, particularly if the books have been obtained from a library, and they return borrowed books promptly, allowing children little long-term access.

It is not easy to employ the informal methods used by effective parents, and it may be unrealistic to think that they can be adopted completely. We need to study exactly what effective parents do and then think carefully about how essential features of these practices can be adapted to classrooms. In the meantime, we fact do not. The evidence denies this, although the methods they use differ significantly from those typically used in schools. Formal reading instruction typically involves the teaching of isolated skills in a predetermined sequence. These procedures are based on the nations that reading must be simplified if children are to understand it and that learning is primarily linear, a matter of gradually building up a associations until everything comes together. Arguments against using reductionist simplification strategies are often based on evidence that some children learn to read before receiving such instruction and that these instances demonstrate that no simplification is necessary and may even be a hindrance.

At issue here are basic assumptions about knowledge. The direct teaching of subskills assumes that knowledge exists in external reality and that learning is a matter of getting what is "out there" into children's heads. However, a different assumption about knowledge is that it exists neither in external reality nor within the learner, but rather is constructed through interactions between the two. if knowledge is derived from actions on objects or experiences. Then a learner must be placed in a situation where such acting can occur. Phonemes do not exist as perceptible units of separate sounds. They "cannot be segmented physically because the acoustic properties of formants of any letter in a syllable are spread across the entire syllable". Our knowledge of distinct sounds does not exist as such in objective reality but is constructed somehow from interactions with speech and print. The problem with much subskill instruction as practiced is that it makes an erroneous assumption about the nature of this knowledge. "Sounds" are regarded as out there" and objective, something children can "hear." When teachers talk about the "sounds" that certain letters make, they may know what they mean, but many children don't.

One reason why children who learn to read with holistic methods before they enter school usually become such good readers may be because they have access to experiences that are complex enough that essential knowledge about the reading process can be derived. But we should not jump too quickly to the assumption that no simplification of the reading situation has been provided. The simplification, however, is not reductionist. A discussion of learning in other areas will serve as an introduction to a discussion of the kind of simplification that may occur.

A complicated form box frustrates children one or one-and-one-half years old. We provide simple form boxes at first. We give children one-piece puzzles at first, too, not ten-piece puzzles. If we misjudge a young child's ability to interact with such materials, however, or if for some reason the child selects a toy too complex, we usually comment on the baby's behavior in sentences such as "He likes to open the lid and put all of the shapes in and then dump them out again," or "Wooden objects are great for teething." Or "Look, he likes to put his fingers through the holes in the lid and then pull it up to see them sticking through the other side. In short, we change our expectations and behavior in relation to the baby and the objects, and the baby copes with the physical objects by doing much more with them than was intended by their designers. And baby, or even an older child in a similar situation, does not become frustrated with being unable to perform the intended task "correctly' because no one demands that it be performed in a certain "fluent" way. In short, we commonly accommodate or "simplify" situations for children by allowing them to add behaviours that are not an essential part of the task for those more experienced.

In addition, parents often add something to the

situation to keep it within the child's realm of experience and ability. We add training wheels to bicycles and thickness to the diameters of pencils and the pages of infant picture books. Perhaps most important, we add social interaction that provides redundancy. This may be especially true of the language we use with very young children Moerk, "What's this? yes, that's your nose. What's this? Yes, that's your mouth. What are these? Uh-huh, those are your eyes. Where are my eyes? Yes, those are my eyes. Where's my nose?" These additions simplify situations, but they do not destroy the essential nature of language, puzzles, bicycles, form boxes, or whatever. They allow children to construct essential knowledge-knowledge perhaps unattainable unless children can act on the "whole ball of wax."

These informal observations and speculations suggest that we might start children on the course of understanding written language by providing "real" reading experiences, but with supports not needed by the mature reader. If we consider storybooks, for example, redundancy is added in a number of ways: rhyme and repetition of phrases make learning the story line easy, pictures support the text and serve as clues to what a page says, and the adult's social behavior of reading the story again and again gives the child a way of knowing what the print says without having had to decipher it. Storybooks seem to fit perfectly the little text, few pages, and uncomplicated plots, do not result in distortion of the essential characteristics of written language: and (2) other simplifications are additions or redundancies, both physical and social. In addition, the situation can be simplified by other additions that consist of information provided by interactions with the adult: "We must start at the from, not the back, of the books": "move your finger; you're covering the words and I can't see to read them": 'wait a minute: I haven't finished reading that page yet": "yes, Max does have a wolf suit on just like it says right here": "you have to point to each word as you say a word, not to each letter, like this. "Finally, the child's knowledge of the story, obtained from having heard it read, provides an important means for discovering mysteries of print-it becomes a monitoring device as was discussed earlier.

Many aspects of reading may be understood only when approached in this manner, for they are complicated rules, to surface structure information. But we will probably not be served well by thinking in dichotomies that suggest that we must simplify situations by cutting them apart or that we must keep them totally complex. Experiences of the sort described above might be called simplified complexities. We need to create and use these in beginning reading instruction.

The roots of literacy are growing strongly long before schools being instruction. Children learn that print represents meaning. They learn general and specific meanings of specific print sequences in situational contexts: stop signs, cereal boxes, toothpaste cartons. At the same time, children develop some awareness of the form of spring: directionality, letter names, key features. They distinguish print from pictures. They can handle books and know the basic function of books, letters, newspapers.

Literacy development in school needs to be built on this base. It must be seen as an extension of natural development.

Literacy development in schools is often not based on "natural" development because the reading behaviors children present upon entrance are not recognized as the precursors of skilled performance in reading and writing. Traditional diagnostic tools often require all-or-none responses: accurate naming of letters or and so on. Most standardized tests are based on reductionist principles that assume precursors of final knowledge to be recognizable, perfect pieces of final knowledge. Errors indicate deficiencies-the absence of specific pieces of knowledge. An F faces to the right, not to the left.

A different view assumes precursors to be qualitatively different from, but nevertheless related to, the final forms of knowledge. The qualitative differences are due to the use of deferent generalizations or rules to organize and manipulate the surface structures of various aspects of language. Errors in this view do not indicate the absence of knowledge but rather the presence of different knowledge. With respect to letter orientation, for example, we can assume that in the beginning many reversals are due to application of a generalization children bring with them from experience with the three-dimensional world: orientation is irrelevant to naming objects: therefore, letters may face any direction, and indeed they do in children's early writing. Somewhat later, children realise that orientation of two-dimensional symbols is meaningful. They then seek rules for orientation by observing letters themselves. If almost all of the left-right asymmetrical letters face right, then all left-right asymmetrical letters must face right, even the J. which, of course is an exception.

This behaviour is similar to a child's assumptions about inflections in oral language: if the past tense of most verbs is formed by adding *ed*, then the past tense of all verbs must be formed in this way, the child reasons. The result is the creation of words such as teached, runned, swinged, and so on. When such errors are assumed to be failures to make discriminations rather than to be applications of different rules, teachers assume children cannot see orientation, that they are unable to perceive it. Training in seeing is often provided, an children are told to look carefully at their writing. But when teachers assume instead that children can see orientation, but have not mastered general rules and their exceptions-that the problem is one of knowing, not perceiving-training in visual discrimination is not provided. Indeed, the problem isn't seen as a problem in need of training at all. it is assumed that these errors will be corrected as children use print more and more jut as errors in oral language are corrected. Instructional activities provided are thus less specific and trivial, and more meaningful and comprehensive.

Errors due to application of different underlying rules by children can also be seen in their early spellings. Children's early categories of sounds are not identical to the categories used by adults. For example, they typically spell words containing *tr* with the letters *ch* because the t preceeding an r is affricated just as ch is. If this phonetic feature, rather than place of articulation, is used as the basis for categorizing sounds, then tr will be considered more closely related to ch than to t as in toy or top. In other words, our categories of phonemes-the distinct sounds we recognize in standard spelling-are not the same as the young child's. Specific developmental stages have been documented for phonological development and its impact on how children spell words which they do not know by sight. In addition, young children generally assume that spelling is phonetic. They have yet to understand that phonetic relations are often violated in standard spelling in order to preserve lexical relationships or similar meanings in words as in nation and nationally, medicine and medical, muscle and muscular. English orthography is based on phonetic and lexical considerations. Young children, however, are "super-phoneticians." "What they discern in the phonetic sequence of spoken words is quite free of higher level 'orthographic overlay, and so they proceed to construct each word by setting out each named letter to its sound".

It is probably a mistake to view children's early spelling as evidence that they know nothing about spelling and to seek to remedy this perceived problem by presenting word lists whose spelling are to be learned one-by one. The problem is of a different order, one of underlying rules and generalizations, one most easily corrected by continued exposure to written words and the need to create them. it seems inefficient tc provide instruction focusing on learning to spell single words when rules relating to many words can be abstracted from broader experiences which would contribute as well to many other literacy skills and keep children meaningfully engaged in, rather than bored with or afraid of, literacy development. The research reviewed here holds much promise for informing us about what is involved in learning to read. Of particular interest are the studies indicating that preschool children who grow up in socially mediated literate environments development. But we need to know more about exactly what these children know and how they develop such knowledge if we are to develop early childhood programs that lead to the same results.

In the meantime, we can attempt to approximate in classrooms both the social and physical environments that appear to foster literacy development in young children. We need to abandon ideas and practices that assume early literacy development to be simply a matter of teaching children a few basic skills such as alphabet recognition or litter-sound associations. Much more is involved. Limiting children's reading experiences to contacts with bits and pieces of print isolated from meaningful contexts may actually prevent them from developing broader and more complex insights that are the key to understanding what writ-classrooms; we need to learn to make it easier. This will require that we provide experiences with real, whole print that we have often assumed in the past to be too complex for young children to understand. We must also learn how to simplify these complexities in ways that don't distort them.

8

Early Childhood Care

The study of individual differences in the organisation of the attachment behaviour illustrates the contribution and limitations of developmental theories for a theory of practice in early education. Bowlby's theory predicts that child care occurring before the fourth phase of attachment will involve a special emotional strain for the child. This strain will be greater when the child is younger and will reflect deficits in the child's rudimentary ability to represent the mother in her absence. A variety of factors including familiarity with the caregiver and the surroundings, the presence of interesting toys, and duration of the separation, also determine the extent of the infant's distress. However, attempts to apply the theory to practical problems often ignore theoretically significant issues. Most attempts at examining the effects of separation due to child care have focused primarily on the fact of the child's enrollment, without attention to the multitude of other factors affecting the child's experience such as age of entrance, length of care, or nature of the care. In one of the earlier studies. Blehar reported that thirty-month-old-day-care children were more avoidant and forty-month-olds more resistant than their age-matched, home-reared controls.

These results have not been replicated by other

researches. The assessment situation used in these studies, however, was developed for use with twelve- to twenty-four-month-olds and so may be inappropriate for assessing attachment in older children. Since the strange situation procedure was inappropriate for the age group examined, these discrepant results are difficult to interpret. In view of Bowlby's analysis, an important issues concerns the influence of day care on the formation of the attachment relationship during the first year of life. Schwartz examined attachment in eighteen-month-old full-time, part-time, and non-day-care infants. The day-care children had been placed in day-care home before six months of age. When the three attendance groups were compared, only 9 per cent of the part-time children were classified as anxiously attached compared to 30 percent of the non-day-care children and 40 percent of the full-time day-care children. Similar group differences were also noted when ratings of avoidant and resistant behaviours were examined. Full-time day-care infants displayed more avoidant behaviour than did their non-day-care or part-time peers. Further, there was a tendency for part-time children to display fewer resistant behaviours than non-day-care children.

Thus, day-care attendance as such did not affect the likelihood that an infant would develop an anxious attachment relationship with the mother. Early enrollment on a full-time basis, however, did result in a greater frequency of behaviour that have been interpreted as signs of suppressed anger at the mother. By contrast, part-time care appears to support the child's bond to the mother. For middle and upper middle class women like those in the present study part-time employment may serve to support their mothering role by offering periods of outside adult contact without the time constraints of full employment. These finding certainly have implications for mothers in-the age of children receiving care. The merits of fill versus part-time employment and the social costs of full versus part-time child care are issues that have personal periods for entry into care. On a basic level this might involve determining which forms of substitute care are appropriate to children in various age groups.

A more subtle issues is whether certain ages, such as ten months of age when attachment behaviours initially appear or eighteen months when there is a sudden reappearance of intense separation protest, might represent crisis points when abrupt introduction to stage surrounding may be disruptive to the child's sense of security. Alternatively, these transitional periods may represent times when the child is ready to make developmental progress and the introduction to day care may facilitate the formation of secondary attachment. Attachment theory also provides a powerful but as yet unrealised analytical tool for studying children's relationships with significant adults other than primary attachment figures. For example, the children in Schwartz's study attended day-care homes with a single alternate caregiver. Infants under one year of age placed with a single adult caregiver have been found to display less resistant behaviours towards the mother than infants cared for in group settings.

Children at this age may not be able to use multiple and changing caregiver effectively as sources of security. Further work needs to be conducted to determine whether various child-care parameters, such as center care, number of substitute caregivers, and group size, differently affect an infant's ability to deal with separation and to form secondary attachments to nonparental adults. Our point is that attachment theory provides a suggestive framework around which applied research can be organised. Although currently the gap between the theory and practical problems is immense, numerous bridging opportunities are available.

While the issues of whether repeated daily separations affect the children's tie to the mother needs further exploration, the inverse, that is, whether the pre-existing attachment tie affects adjustment to day care and interactions with peers or caregivers, has received slim attention. A few recently completed studies have examined the relationship between the quality of the attachment bond and later social behaviours with peers. These studies indicate a relationship between secure attachment and subsequent social competence. As part of a longitudinal study, securely attached children were found to display greater task persistence and longer periods of exploration at twenty-four months. These children were rated higher on scales of peer competence and ego strength at age three and a half and scored higher at ages four and five on measures of curiosity.

In another sample, securely attached three-year-olds displayed more signs of peer competence than their anxiously attached peers. Even though secure attachment may promote social competence in laboratory settings or at later ages in school, it is unclear whether a similar relationship holds for younger children in day care where other factors such as the stress of separation might be expected to affect behaviour as well. Further, the implications for anxiously attached children's adjustment to day care needs to be explored.

On the one hand, separations from the mother are thought to heighten anxiety in these children. On the other day-care-experience has been found to promote peer competence. In the long run, day may be beneficial for anxiously attached children if the setting promotes satisfying relationships with adults and peers. Investigations of individual differences in the quality of attachment might consider the process by which children use the substitute caregiver as a secure base as well as the quality of that relationship. Similar inquiries might also examine whether anxious secure attachment relationships with the mother are mirrored in the relationship with the caregiver. Apparently, children are able to sue substitute caregivers for security when under stress in new situations and many even do so with a stranger.

Although there is a good deal of information on the conditions under which infants form secure attachment bonds to the mother, little is known about the formation and the nature of attachment bonds with new caregivers and the conditions under which these attachments optimally occur. For a theory of practice, information about such issues is essential. The process by which young children are introduced to child care may have a major influence on their ability to perceive the setting as a secure environment. Early childhood educators have long struggled with the issue of initial adjustment periods and methods to bring about a sense of familiarity. Using a minimalist approach. Schwatz and Wynn found that an initial visit to the center by the mother and child had little effect on later adjustment, but the visit was brief and exposure to the new adult was minimal. A maximalist approach would frame the issue somewhat differently. Suppose maternal presence in the center provides the child with a secure base to explore and become familiar with other children and adults. Suppose also that some of these individuals eventually become able to functions as supports for the child when the mother leaves. A maximalist approach might attempt to identify the time span within which most children are able to form sufficiently robust secondary attachments to facilitate the transition.

A teacher who has visited the child at home several times, a familiar peer, or a sibling may, separately or in combination, serve to smooth the transition period. Numerous other factors such as the level of cooperation and understanding between mother and caregiver, the mother's way of managing the separation or the warmth and skill of the caregiver probably contribute in some measure to ameloriating distress. Our point is simply that a theory of practice must identify controllable aspects of the environment which in various combinations make a difference for most children. As currently formulated, attachment theory offers some clues but few guides for what these aspects might be.

Children spend a substantial amount of time and energy exploring their environment. But this environment is not a neutral force. Some environments are relatively barren and offer little enticement. Others are excessively stimulating and overwhelm children rather than entice them.

Although Berlyne's arousal theory of curiosity and

exploration is less well developed than attachment theory, it provides a useful framework for considering the influence of the physical environment on child behaviour. If attachment theory implies that a secure base facilitates exploratory behaviour, arousal theory implies that some environments are more explorable than others.

According to Berlyne, there are at least two types of exploratory behaviour, specific and diversive that differ in the way they are tied to environmental events. Specific exploration occurs when the individual is disturbed by a "lack of information, and thus left prey to uncertainty and conflict".

A lack of information occurs when the individual encounters stimulation that is novel, surprising, ambiguous, incongruous, complex, or in other ways too difficult to assimilate easily. Specific exploration supplies the "precise information" that the individual misses. Berlyne uses the term "curiosity" to describe the condition of discomfort that motivates specific exploration. By contrast, diversive exploration occurs when the environment is too familiar, too predictable, and too easy to assimilate. Under these conditions, individuals seek out stimulation to alleviate boredom. But sometimes stimulation is in excess; the environment is too novel, too ambiguous, too complex, or too unpredictable. Instead of eliciting approach and contact, these environments may elicit fear and withdrawal.

The glue binding these behaviours is provided by the construct of arousal, a motivating state that can be too low, too high, or just might. When the individual's level of arousal departs from a comfortable optimum, the individual engages in exploration or avoidance until the optimum is restored. The concept of an optimum is conceptualised by Berlyne as a transient state defined by the absence of uncertainty, boredom, or fear. Some of the problems posed by a definition "by absence" will be discussed below. First, however, it is helpful to examine how Berlyne's theory pertains to problems in early education. Several studies have examined children's behaviour with materials varying in complexity. Two of these seem especially informative with respect to the physical characteristics of early childhood environments likely to sustain children's interest.

In one study the investigators, constructed two play settings varying in complexity. The low-complexity setting consisted of two large trestles, one medium-sized trestle, a balance beam, four mats, a slide, a bench, and a chair. The high-complexity setting included all of the above and, in additions, a metal ladder and a rope spanning the two large trestles, five wooden panels and three ropes attached to each of the trestle, and two wooden boxes and four wooden cubes arranged underneath the trestles. Over a period of three consecutive weeks, two groups of ten children were exposed to each setting for fifteen minutes a day. The investigators asked, first, whether children would prefer the more complex setting to the less complex one and, second, whether this interest would be sustained over successive days. The results were relatively straightforward. The children showed a higher level of engagement with the more complex apparatus. Over the three-week period, their engagement with the each type of apparatus dropped, but at the end of three weeks, the children still preferred the more complex apparatus.

Clearly, with repeated exposure, children's interest in even attractive play equipment will diminish. There is also evidence that children's waning interests can be recharged. In one study, changing half the items in a toy set increased children's interest in the toys. Berlyne's theory and the findings that follow from it suggest that a theory of practice might need to include rules for producing complexity and variation in the classroom setting. But the level of complexity and variation that is attractive will depend on the age of the child. Properly speaking, Berlyne's theory is not a theory of development. There are no specific provisions in the theory for statements about developmental change either in the form of exploratory behaviour or in elements of the environments likely to attract children at different ages. However, the theory does suggest that as children encounter stimulation, their ability to process environmental information will improve. Older children are expected to prefer higher levels of novelty, and to be less likely to be fearful of new or complex events.

However, for any particular event, preference, boredom, or avoidance will depend on the child's prior experiences. Unfortunately, the theory has not developed to the point of being able to identify in advance which events are likely to be more or less familiar or understood. However, the idea that children's response to such events will vary as a functions of age is consistent with the evidence. For example, there is some evidence that young children may avoid excessive complexity. In one study, children were presented two-dimensional vinyl shapes varying in complexity according to the number of turns on the edges. In two-year-olds, exploratory behaviour increased from low to moderate levels of stimulus complexity but when declined. By contrast, in four-to seven-year-olds, exploratory behaviour reached its highest level with the most complex objects. The message of the study is that a level of complexity that encourages exploration in older children may discourage it in younger children. An activity that intrigues a four-year-old may overwhelm a two-year-old. Although the study of exploratory behaviour has been far less richly detailed than the study of attachment behaviour, it nonetheless offers some clues for the inter-pretation of young children's behaviour. Consider, for example, a three-years-old's first day in a group program. It is play time and block buildings are being built and toppled, several children are playing a game with the slide, others are working puzzles, finger painting, or just moving from activity to activity watching what the others are doing. The room is noisy and the 15 children are active and engaged.

Sally clings to her mother. But her eyes scan the room. She watches a group modeling with clay. In one corner of the room, two children have a tussle, and one of the cries. Sally watches the teacher settle the dispute with intense interest. Her eyes move to a corner of the room where a group of children have knocked over a tower. She smiles in response to their laughter. Her mother whispers something in her ear and gets up as if to leave. Sally clutches her mother's dress and protests. Her mother sits down. Sally and her mother stay for the rest of the morning but Sally never leaves her mother's side.

Over the next few days Sally gingerly begins to explore the environment, but always with a watchful eye on her mother. The teacher is able to interest her in play dough or a toy, and she begins to wander around the room pausing to observe various activities. At first, these tours are brief followed by hasty returns to her mother. Gradually, they become longer, but distress appears at the slightest sign of the mother's departure.

Attachment theorists might say that Sally's problem is in separating from the parent. Yet, she has little difficulty staying with babysitters or relatives, in her own home or in other homes, even in those that are relatively unfamiliar. But in the classroom, she seems to be under considerable stress. Arousal theorists might say that the sources of stress is in the classroom environment not in the child. The group setting is not novel but excessively complex. Fifteen children and three adults offer more behavioural possibilities than the child can possibly predict; too many things happen too unexpectedly. There is more information in the environment than the child can process and so she clings to the mother, a source of stability and predictability. The child's observing behaviour, her tentative, exploratory jaunts, serve to reduce the uncertainty. But the process of uncertainty reduction takes time; it is facilitated by a secure and predictable source of comfort.

This argument has some provocative and verifiable implications for a practical theory of environmental transitions. For example, a new child might be introduced to something like a decompression chamber. This chamber might be simply a protected play vestibule near the door of the class room, a space richly equipped with attractive toys, a friendly teacher, and only few children. The purpose of the decompression chamber is to contain the uncertainty of a new environment by presenting it in more manageable chunks. Children introduced to the group setting in such a way might be expected to explore more freely; to leave the mother sooner, and to protest less when the mother departs. Consider another type of child, one who has been attending a group program for almost two years. The following is not an unusual observation. Len sits down at the painting table. He picks up a brush and quickly dabs color on the paper. Then he gets up and wanders over to the housekeeping area, pausing briefly to pot on the stove before moving on to the blocks. There he takes a car away from Jimmy who cries "No," Len smiles and puts the car behind his back. Jimmy grabs for the car and the two begin to wrestle. The teacher breaks it up and returns the car to Jimmy. Len moves along looking for something else to do.

The teachers describe Len's behaviours as restless and aimless. They feel that he is easily distracted and that his attention span is short. He frequently disrupts other children's activity and initiates rough-and-tumble or running games. One day, the teacher brings a water table into the room. The new materials has a striking effect on Len's behaviour; the restlessness, aimlessness, and seemingly undirected behaviour disappear. He is totally absorbed in the water activity, systematically examining the varied objects and exploring the effects produced by combinations of water with things. Len's behaviour on the first day involved largely sensory-motor manipulations. By the third day, pretend play appeared, and the ideational quality of Len's behaviour changed. According to arousal theorists, Len's aimless wandering can be interpreted as a response to boredom. The tussle with Jimmy offered a source of relief, except that it was not a permitted activity. The water table provided a pleasant level of novelty and the possibilities it offered sustained Len's interest for several days. In an attempt to refine arousal theory, Nunnally and Lemond proposed a sequential model of exploratory behaviour. According to this model, an interesting event produces heightened attention followed by specific exploration. The object is explored or manipulated until uncertainty concerning its physical properties is reduced. Uncertainty reduction is followed by pretense or some other form of play identified with autistic thinking. Finally, boredom sets in, the individual sets off in search of stimulation, and the sequence repeats itself. The advantages of the Nunnally and Lemon model is that it introduces a role for play as distinct from exploration, but for the most part, the behavioural categories employed by arousal theorists are fairly global. Neither the stimulus properties that attract children's interest not the behaviours they engage in have been sufficiently specified to offer more than a suggestive framework for a theory of practice. The theory's limitations do, however, illustrate the need for a developmental theory of attractive environments.

In Berlyne's theory of exploratory behaviour, individuals seek out objects or experiences for their own sake rather than for rewards arbitrarily associated with such activity. According to this view, the motivation for activity is built into the activity itself. If intrinsic motivation were part of a theory of practice, emphasis would be more on the inherently appealing activities or materials practitioners might offer children than on systems of external rewards or inducements. In Berlyne's theory, intrinsic motivation is conceptualised as the alleviation of aversive states. For a more positive perspective, it is necessary to turn to White's notion of mastery motivation which owes much to the work of Piaget.

Suppose an infant notices the movement of a toy parrot suspended above his crib. Soon after, the infant discovers that deliberate body movements will control the toy's movements. According to Berlyne, the moving parrot provokes the child's curiosity; he explores the parrot until sufficient information is gained and uncertainty is reduced. But this explanation does not account for the seeming goal-orientedness of the behaviour. The baby's exploration is not haphazard and exploration is not a simple matter of visual or tactile contact. Rather, something special happens when the child discovers the contingency between his behaviour and an event. This discovery seems to have its own special reward. According to Piaget, the infant has a special capacity to detect such contingencies and to perceive them as causally connected. The child interprets the contingency as evidence of control and derives a feeling of efficacy from successful efforts to control the environment. According to this view, children not only are motivated to recognise a challenge when it is presented to them, but they also seek out optimally challenging situations. Suppose children are presented a range of problems, some easy, some middling, and some hard. Which problems will children choose, and which will give them the most pleasure? Recent evidence suggests that children will choose moderately difficult problems, even when more pleasure from mastering the moderately difficult problems, even when more difficult problems can be solved. Moreover, they derive more pleasure from mastering the moderately difficult challenges undermine the feelings of pleasure that come with mastery. These findings highlight what we already know; survival in a harsh world may enhance one's feeling of competence without necessarily bringing joy and pleasure. The evidence suggests that in a theory of practice, there may be a need for statements about the diversification of challenges and the child's freedom to choose those best matched to his or her ability. Unfortunately, the research has not clarified how the relation between ability and problem might be specified in advance. And although Piaget's theory has provided much of the basis for the concept of mastery, its structural account of development challenging at different developmental levels. As we indicated earlier, the minimalist orientation of developmental theory tends to reduce the importance of such a specification. By contrast, a theory of practice requires rules for assessing children's level of ability with respect to different types of challenges. In this case, the requirements of a theory of practice may exert an independent force for the extension and, perhaps, revision of developmental theory.

Research on intrinsic motivation has yielded additional information of interest to a theory of practice. On the one hand, much of what children do is done because they derive intrinsic pleasure from activity, But on the other, adults often add external rewards in the form of approval, gold stars, or special treats. What happens when intrinsic and extrinsic rewards are mixed? Not surprisingly, the effect depends on the particular children involved. Suppose, for example, that preschool children are divided into two groups who have either a high or a low spontaneous interest in drawing. Now suppose that half the children in each interest group are offered a prize for drawing and the other half are not. Even though the experimental session is brief, rewarded children who initially had a high interest in drawing will, a week later, show less interest than high-interest children who received no extrinsic reward. Children who find an activity intrinsically challenging "turn off" when given prizes for doing what they ordinarily do for its own sake. Moreover, during the reward sessions, the quality of the children's drawings decrease, as if the intrinsic pleasure of combining lines and colors had been replaced by another sources of excitement. A strikingly different effect appeared in children who initially showed little spontaneous interest in drawing. A week after the reward session, these children demonstrated an increased interest in drawing during the free-play period. Changes in the behaviours of these children seemed to follow the rule that extrinsic reinforcement will increase the behaviour upon which it is contingent. But changes in the behaviour of the high-interest children suggest that this rule does not always apply. According to Lepper *et al* extrinsic reward may undermine children's intrinsic motivation because the basis of the activity changes from the intrinsic, "I do it because it's fun to make nice pictures" to the extrinsic "I do it because it will get me a prize." The shift to extrinsic reward also leads to less complex, less creative, and less refined drawings, as if the introduction of external rewards also undermines the internal standard of excellence so essential to the pursuit of mastery. A number of theoretical formulations have been developed to account for children's response to aspects of the environment such as novelty, complexity, or challenge. These formulations advance a common notion, namely, that much human activity is sustained by satisfactions inherent in an individual's transactions with the environment. These formulations also clarify differences in the way intrinsic motivation might be conceptualised. Arousal theory points to general features of the environment, whereas mastery theory points to the availability of developmentally appropriate problems. A theory of practice, especially in early education, might require statements about each of these environmental domains. it may even be that rules about the provision of developmentally appropriate problems will help to specify more precisely the meaning of novelty, complexity, and similar variables.

The concept of mastery motivation is addressed to the general problem of why children acquire skills and learn to solve problems in the absence of social or appetitising pressure. But interesting thing happen after a skill has been acquired. A young child learns go down a slide with much effort; each steep step is slowly mounted, and during the first few trips, the child holds tightly and apprehensively to the sides. Within a few days, the same child goes down the slide in all sorts of complicated ways, rocking, clapping, kicking, singing, back-ways, belly-ways, head first, with a friend, a toy, or some combination of these. These ways of maneuvering an inclined plane are repeated, elaborated, recombined, and varied.

Piaget uses the term practice play to designate activities in which the child creates deliberate complications and seems to make things purposefully difficult. In a mastery activity under the control of a goal, means are marshaled in the service of an end. But in play, means are repeated, elaborated, and become a sources of interest in their own right. Miller refers to these elaborations of means as "Galumphing." According to Miller, behaviour oriented toward ends becomes efficient and streamlined over time; the child can go up and down the slide with few unnecessary or wasted movements. But after mastery, what next? In developing Piaget's notion of play as a postmastery behaviour. Miller argues that its pleasure come neither from environmental challenge nor from arousal stimulated by a novel or unknown object. Rather, the pleasure comes from the child's control over arousal through the production of diversity, regardless of its particular form. Play involves a relative autonomy of means which implies a degree of autonomy for the player. Miller's notion of "galumphing" as a "patterned, voluntary elaboration or complication of process, where the pattern is not under the dominant control of goals" is entirely in keeping with Piaget's notion of play as assimilation. In Piagetian theory, assimilation refers to the process whereby the child imposes his own way of thinking on the world. Accommodation, by contrast, refers to the process whereby the child's organisations is adjusted to meet the world's demands. In mastery activities, assimilation and accommodation operate synchronously-the child behaves according to what he understands; if the behaviour and goal is attained. In the example given earlier, the infant might smile at the parrot to make it move; if smiling does not work, some other behaviour will be tried until behaviours which reliably move the parrot are found. Assimilation refers to previously acquired action patterns brought to bear on the current problem; accommodation refers to the behavioural adjustments needed to solve the problem. In play, assimilation dominates accommodation, there is asynchrony rather than synchrony. Action patterns are produced and varied without much regard to a particular goal. According to Piaget, "play proceeds by the relaxation of the effort at adaptation" The pleasure comes from a feeling of super-mastery a "feeling of virtuosity or power". Play, then, represents a special type of challenge. It is not a type of challenge presented by the environment nor is it is type of challenge sought in the environment. Play represents challenge produced by the child, and as such it offers a special type of developmental opportunity. As one of the authors has noted elsewhere, pretend play illustrates this assimilative mode at a symbolic level. Symbolic play extends the sensory-motor play of an earlier period. Rather than actually going down the slide a hundred ways, the child may make a toy animal go down in ways that for the child would be physically impossible or even disastrous. The toy animal can hop down, leap down, or even fall down. The child can slide down hugging a "frightened" baby doll, turn the slide into a hill for cars, or initiate numerous other activities which transcend the literal meaning of a solid object on an inclined plane.

Pretend play as assimilation also implies that means/ends relations have been temporarily severed. What at an earlier period were means are now meanings. During the sensory-motor period, going down the slide head-first was just that; a novel, challenging, slightly scary way of doing a familiar activity. Now the same behaviour might represent a down-hill ride on a sled, a plane coming in for a landing, or a trip to the Moon. At an earlier level of development, the slide was a slide, the child was his real self, and the activity occurred in a world of tangible objects. Now, either the slide, the child, or any other feature of the environment can be transformed. According to Piaget, the special pleasure of symbolic play comes from the child's ability to manipulate and very meanings as well as means.

In discussing attachment theory, we noted that one of its values for teachers and parents is that it marks behaviours that reveal how children feel about people and social situations.

The theory offers an interpretive framework within which behaviours such as smiles, eye-eye contact, and proximity along with their opposites-frowns, gaze avoidance and distance-hold privileged positions as indicators of children's affectional ties and feelings of comfort and security. In discussing theories of arousal and mastery, we argued that these formulations had more to say about the quality of children's environments than about the quality of their behaviour.

The notion of galumphing, especially if placed in the context of Piagetian theory, returns us once again to behaviour. At a sensory-motor level of behaviour, play activities develop from activities with a single object to those involving combinations of two or more objects. The overall pattering of object behaviour changes as well. Between the ages of eighteen and twenty-four months, children contact more diverse elements of the environment, and as they so do, the tendency to get struck on one particular object diminishes. Pretense, too, changes in systematic ways. Initially, the child produces the motions of sleeping without intending to sleep or the motions of eating without intending to eat. These activities seem to take place outside their customary context and seen divorced from their customary functions of rest and nourishment. Over the next year and a half, these ephemeral gestures become elaborated and enriched. At first, a doll is simply an object to be touched, moved, or banged. Somewhat later, the doll is used as the recipient of food and eventually is made the recipient of a complex array of care-giving activities, it is put to bed, dressed, patted, and spanked. The child's voice quality might change to sound like a parent, gestures, clothing, and other element might combine to indicate that a role enactment is occurring. At first, the objects used in pretense tend to be similar to the things used in the real life situations that pretend activities mimic. Gradually, the need for verisimilitude weakens and assorted objects can be used as substitutes in pretend enactments. Eventually, the child can create the semblance of a physical entity. Initially, pretend play is a solo activity. Adults may participate and organise it, but children under three years of age rarely share pretend sequences with one another except, perhaps, in brief, imitative, parallel exchanges. By two-and-a-half years of age, the beginning of sociodramatic play appear and, by the age of five years, what began as a few simple gestures encompasses intricate systems of reciprocal roles, ingenious improvisations of materials, increasingly coherent themes, and weaving plots.

Sociodramatic play also demonstrates a systematic pattern of developmental changes. At first, children communicate primarily about their own roles. Later, they discuss others' roles and the activities that will be engaged in during the play.

There are also changes in the types of role relationships enacted. At first, role relationships tend to be those in which the children have participated in real life, and only later do these encompass the role relationships observed in others. The social organisation of the play changes as well. At three, children are more likely to engage in complementary role play in which differentiated roles are assigned, but in the play these roles are enacted independently. Older children are more likely to produce integrative role structures in which the activity of each player is tied to the activity of the others and the roles are constituted through reciprocal relationships between the players.

Information about the development of play behaviour and sensitive observation of behaviour provide clues to children's level of cognitive and social maturity. More important, this information can serve as the basis for attempts to enhance or elaborate the play. A major contribution to a theory of teaching practice can be found in Smilansky's detailed analysis of how teachers might proceed from a careful assessment of children's current level of play to a set of systematic strategies for enriching the thematic context of the play children's skills at using play techniques.

Play is also enhanced by features of the physical environment. With respect to a theory of practice, several of these features are under the practitioner's control. Depending on the children's developmental level, realistic prop might be more supportive of play than abstract materials. According to Nunnally and Lemon, novelty might enhance exploratory behaviour, but familiarity might enhance play. A play space protected from unpredictable intrusions, familiar peers, and unpressured time are other factors likely to enhance play. Further progress toward a theory of practice will require more intensive study of how teachers and others can create optimal conditions for play. As this issues is addressed, abstractions such as novelty or familiarity will require rules for their actual production, rules which then might yield examples of environmental variation currently unavailable to theories of development.

Is it important to have play as part of the preschool curriculum? Must play be part of a theory of practice in early education? So far, the evidence favors a positive response to both questions. Pretend play, for examples, is associated with the combinatorial flexibility that characterises creative thinking. Although children must have some skills in taking the perspective of others in order to engage in sociodramatic play, there is evidence that these skills are consolidated when children engage in such play. Numerous studies indicate that sociodramatic play has a positive influence on perspective taking and cooperation. Although the process responsible for this influence is not understood, the evidence indicates that activity in an assimilative mode deepens children's grasp of physical and social phenomena. If creativity and social sophistication are considered desirable developmental outcomes, play becomes a practical means whereby these outcomes can be promoted.

As Bronfenbrenner astutely noted, a theory of practice creates a demand for an ecological theory of human development. According to our analysis, such a theory will assume the maximalist orientation traditionally adopted by theories of practice and traditionally rejected by theories of development. Brofenbrenner's proposal in effect requires a massive revision of the form of developmental theory. Consider, for example, the way attachment theory has dealt with affectional relations. For numerous reasons, the focus of the theory has been consistently on the child's developing relationship with the particular person, who functions as the primary caregiver during the first year of life. In a theory of practice, this focus must expand. For a theory of parenting for example, the focus must shift to the parent's developing relationships with the child, and include the parent's perception of the social and material resources that impinge upon that relationship. Put another way a theory of parenting must consider the parent's perceptions of the child's perceptions of significant social and material resources. But such a theory must also consider the parent's perceptions of a broader domain, along with rules for mobilising that domain to serve the best interests of the developing child as determined by the values held by the parent.

At the heart of a theory of practice are statements about how controllable resources are to be obtained and allocated. These statements have enormous implications for an ecologically sensitive and valid theory of development. At one time, development theory rested almost exclusively on studies in which the experimental situation was rigged so as to demonstrate almost any possibility. These situations have been properly criticised as artificial, first, because they are likely to be perceived as ersatz even by children, and second, because they often bizarrely distort physical and social events. More recently, there has been a shift in emphasis from rigged to actual environments. But actual environments are inherently opaque because the rigging is obscure. To the extent that principles derived from a theory of practice permit conceptions of actualisable environments developmental theory will be able to consider realisable possibilities.

Attachment theory offers one illustration of the pressure of practice forcing maximalist expansion in a theory of development. Theories of exploration and play illustrate a different type of pressure. In the case of arousal theory, concept of complexity or novelty are to general to serve the needs if practice without additional elaboration. In a theory of development, it is necessary too formulate rules for reducing the immense diversity and variability of the world into general categories; when applied, these rules transform particulars into potentially universal dimensions. These rules make it possible to define complexity as the number of movable parts in a climbing apparatus or as the number of turns in a vinyl object. But in a theory of practice, universal dimensions must be transformed into particulars; the rules of practice are generative rather than reductive. These rules will be restricted to the particular domain of resources controlled by a given practitioner, but they will be stated so that with in the domain an immense variety of concrete examples can be generated. If complexity and novelty are crucial physical dimensions governing the exploratory behaviour of children and if this behaviour is deemed a desirable goal for practice then a theory of practice must contain rules fir generating environments that ate appropriately complex or novel.

The theory if mastery motivation illustrates another problem. To date, this theory has not taken full advantage if the development theory from which it was derived. The theory is unnecessarily overgeneralised, omitting the voluminous literature specifying qualitative changes in the nature if children's thinking. From the perspective of practice, this omission offers an instance in which development theory has not taken full advantage of its own potential. A proper theory of mastery requires evidence of the way in which children in the natural environment define and solve problems as a functions of their level of cognitive development. With this evidence in had, a theory if practice can construct procedural statements based on the practitioner's identification of children's cognitive level and the specification of developmentally appropriate challenges.

Finally, there is the message offered by Piaget's notion if play as assimilation. Although the notion of assimilation in this special sense has had its strongest application to the play of young children, it has implications for adult thought that have yet to be explored. According to Piaget, personal and imaginal symbolism is required by adults to concretise abstract thought. In piaget's words; "The minds which are best able to control abstractions are those which succeed in embodying them in concrete examples... which then serve as symbolic springboards without introducing any limitations". In the division of labor implied by the separation of theories of development from theories of practice, it may fall to the practitioner to generate concrete examples from developmental abstractions. If this is a, major task of a theory of practice is to consider formulations about the creative and imaginative potential of the practitioner. But Piaget's insight also suggests that the current radical separation between these types of theory might operate to the disadvantage of progress in each. At the very least, a deliberate recognition of mutual dependency may contribute to more adaptive theories in each domain.

9

Child Care and Education

Many people use the words "traditional child-care" in a different way. To mean "care within the institution of a nuclear family. For these people nontraditional care then means care in an institution different from the nuclear family say a commune or day care centre or a 24 hour state nursery or a household following death or divorce or a lesbian household. On the other hand will use the words "traditional child care" to mean responsibility for children and care of young children by women. Under circumstances where men would find it difficult to care for those children and where only women would be comfortable doing so in our society. Thus day-care and 24 hour state centers. Foster care, care by divorcees, and lesbian households might all be "traditional child care" in my sense, if the female child carers perceive themselves to be constrained by sex-role stereotypes so powerful that neither hey nor would be male child cares have the freedom to negotiate who will carte for the children. By the same token, androgynous child care according to the definitions of this paper, might occur in families, centers and other institutions and occurs wherever both men and wome have equal options to negotiate with themselves and each other on who will care for children.

About four-fifths of American households with children under 14 are in nuclear family form About 90% of all households with children under 14 now use some kind of care at some time in a given week; more than half use care more than an hour per week; about a quarter use a child-care arrangement 10 or more hours per week; about eighth use care 30 or more hours per week. The main types of care are relatives in one's own or another home or a nonrelative in one' own home or another home. Day-care centers, cooperative programs nurseries and preschools, and before and after-school programs together comprise at most a 10th of all arrangements. About two-thirds of all households pay no cash for child but many arrangements are reimbursed in kind only about a 10th of all arrangements are considered "free'.

Multiple arrangements are very common, with over half of all care-using households reporting the father as a regular supplementary caretaker three-tenths regularly using an older sibling and an eighth regularly leaving children alone, in addition to the relatives and nonrelatives and formal care reported above as " main types of care. 'Hours that children are in school after school are also an important "child care arrangement for two ninths of all children under 14.

Of interest to the present discussion we find fathers estimated as fewer than 10% of all main types of child carers but they are clearly helping out significantly, as noted above. How much are men becoming involved in child care? There is scattered evidence of the importance of men as child cares in some specific groups of the population. For instance, among the families of professional psychologists, roughly a sixth to a quarter of the care of the children is reported to be by husbands with nonspouse arrangements on the same order of magnitude, and mothers caring for children 60% to 70% of the time. The Michigan Survey Research Center study of 5,000 American families is also reported to have found many men comparably engaged in child care. And about 8% of all children under 18 years who were reported living in nonnuclear tamilies were in nonnuclear families headed by a male in 1974.

On the other hand, time budget studies of several years ago showed that employed mothers spent seven to 10 hours more per week on total work and work-related activities than did employed fathers. And the "extra time devoted by employed mothers was predominantly in child care and homemaking. Moreover, there is some reason to believe that fathers on the average, got more sleep and hand more time in leisure activities than did mothers. The mothers in fact appeared to get less than optimal sleep on a regular basis. Some evidence has indicated that the amount of time spent by employed fathers on child care and homemaking depended primarily on what these men were otherwise doing it did not depend very much on whether the mother had a paid job or on the number of children in the family. On the other hand, some studies appear to indicate that husbands/fathers have performed a little more housework and child care when wives/mothers are employed, the increase usually expressed as an increase in the percent of total homemaking taken on by the husband. My own experience also indicate that many women believe this is the case. However, we believe that the major shift that occurs when a wife/mother takes a paid job is that the total amount of family work time drops very sharply and that because the husband's family work time stays nearly the same he is doing a larger proportion of the homemaking.

Of course these statistics on child-care arrangements tell us nothing certain about the attitudes of the child cares and the extent to which they are or feel constrained by sex role stereotyping. But we find fathers as primary care givers for only a few percent of American children and mothers as the primary care gives for nearly half of all U.S. children. Moreover most mothers retain basic responsibility for children most of the time, and seven-eighths of all households use nonmaternal care only 30 hours per week of less out of the 168 hours in a week. it is easy therefore to hypothesize that serious sex-role stereotyping with respect to children is very important in the U.S.

Comparable statistics do not exist for other countries. We know that, in predominantly rural areas of the world it is usually women who care for children at home or at work and usually together with other women, or that older children care for younger children under the eye of a nearby adult. In other industrialized nations more like our own, sex-role differentiation appears to be as common as in the United States. In the Soviet Union, top government officials will say, we believe women to be better suited to child care. Soviet fathers are kept out of maternity hospitals and have no paternity leave the first year of their child's life and practically no men are involved in the day to day formal care that affects perhaps 40% Soviet urban preschoolers and in Israel comparable sex role differentiation obtains. Only in United States and Scandinavia do we find significant if small proportions of men involved in formal child care. And only in

Scandinavia and Cuba top government leaders systematically asserted equal rights for men in the home and with children and equal sharing with women of social responsibility for reproducing and socializing the human species. Nowhere does that equal sharing appear yet to have taken place.

Support for traditional practices and policies has generally rested on two grounds. First it is asserted that women are biologically better able to care for children and that men are hormonally and morphologically better able to support a family. Second it is asserted that a whole socioeconomic system has been erected on the basis of the biological differences and that this system is a good thing because sex role differentiation has been effective and efficient in getting done the work of the world. It is my point of view that differences in child rearing capabilities and requirements formerly did mean that women were better adapted to child care but that biological differences with respect to parenting no longer have much meaning in this era of zero population growth, planned parenthood, and bottle feeding. Hormonal and morphologic differences in men may also have meant that males were in some societies better provides in an age hunting and frontier life. We believe that this is not generally true in our services-oriented economy where cooperation and human organization are so exceptionally important. I believe that the traditional social and economic sex role differentiation is no longer helpful to industrialized society and that androgyny offers a more effective and humane system for child care as well as for other employment.

Effects on children

Many experts in recent years have surveyed the evidence concerning the effect on children of different child care arrangements. Extensive and exhaustive these reviews regularly conclude that stable responsive consistent care is important indeed critical to young children. Recent studies also conclude that care of this nature can be delivered by a variety of different kinds of people. Men and women, teenagers and grandparents, single and multiple attachment figures in a variety of settings. Although questions have been raised about the effect of 24 hour care on children in institutions in kibbutzim or in 24 hour centers in the Soviet Union or about the effects of too much violent television by and large it is very difficult to demonstrate long-term effects on children from any kind of nonabusive care and education arrangement. The public consensus in the United States also appears to be swinging toward a belief that child cars may help socialize children, especially those in small families. And that parental employment and child care may make children more independent. it seems reasonable to conclude that many types of arrangements are suitable for children, where the environment is safe and supportive and there are consistent warm, responsive stable attachment figures as caretakers.

On the other hand, numerous observers believe that families need more support that children are happier when they see more their fathers, and that children might be happier with several different parental figures to turn to instead of depending exclusively on overworked isolated mothers. And many people are deeply concerned by the number of children under the age 10 who are now regularly left alone or who are in abusive care situations numbers which may total 10% or more of our young children.

Effects women and men

Our traditions about women and children bring great joy and happiness to many men and women. Others have for decades ignored the traditions equally happily. Still others were brought up in different traditions were women shared financial responsibility and/or men shared in all nurturance activities many of these people and their families have also thrived.

There are many women and men, however, who are not happy either ignoring the modal tradition or living within it. And still others are happy for years with traditional sex roles and then feel constrained and confined and frustrated and bewildered. In this discussion we will concentrate on the difficulties with traditional roles with respect to child care since we are concerned mainly with providing options. The ensuing discussion presents what we see as negative consequences of our present child care arrangements. In a larger sense these consequences are due to the whole pattern of sex role stereotyping rather than just to child care. And as we noted above there may be several reasons why sex role differentiation occurred in the first place. At present however we believe that child care arrangements have come to symbolize all the reasons for sex roles: they constitute perhaps the most powerful remaining institutionalization of our stereotypes. it is in this sense then that one present some consequences of sex role differentiation in the context of consequences of child care arrangements. The Sense of Separateness of men and Women. The presumption that children and family were women's work has, we believe led through our early socialization patterns to an extraordinary segregation of most men's lives from most women's lives. Especially in industrialized societies. In our own work we are continually impressed by the extent to which men and women do not understand each other's experience.

More damaging yet is the frequent presumption that at base men and women cannot ultimately understand each other or live the same life style. Liberal men will often support the entrance of women into say engineering, But then if someone asks about men in child care. This same liberal may ask. But could men really take care of children as well as women? The soviet Union and china assert complete equality for women. These countries have however, desegregated only lower and middle level male occupations leaving child care and homemaking as segregated as ever. Conservative and radical women also often speak as if only women could care for children. We are all accustomed to hearing very conservative women speak this way but it is sometimes as true radical women. Revolutionary feminists deplore the oppression of women which may result from woman's traditional child care responsibilities but them some radical feminists turn to discussions of gestation in test tubes and of child care in 24 hour day care centers in a way which appears by exclusion to accept the notion that fathers and children might damage each other's lives. In others words, some feminists reject the oppression of individual women, but then turn to day care as if it were an improvement. Some improvement may in fact occur the caretakers are usually paid and sometimes have each other to talk with but the traditional sex role pattern obtains.

Another result of traditional thinking is that large numbers of men and women including sadly some parents, have concluded that children and or child care is too much for them. For example, Ann Landers recently reported that 70% of 10.000 parents who noted her about having children reported that they would not do it again. And a recent Gallup Poll reported that one in 10 of all mothers randomly surveyed "regretted having children".

Loneliness. Present child-care arrangements are lonely for many parents. Isolated mothers and paid caretakers are often lonely, men who commute and do not see their families are often lonely. Marriages in which one spouse is a homemaker, working 99 hours per week and the other works overtime or moonlights up to 80-90 hours per week are hard on communications. The disproportionate numbers of depressed young mothers illuminate the sadness of spouses with not enough chance to be with those they love.

Moreover in many of the shared parenting arrangements that now exist the parents both work full time in paid jobs with one or both in charge of the children during hours when the parent should be sleeping. Here the parents share care sometimes at the price of sleep. However, since our society as a whole is set up for paid workers without child-care responsibilities the parents may be able to earn two incomes only by staggering their work hours. This means that, in may two-job families one parent is with the children primarily when the children are sleep and also that the parents have little waking or sleeping time together.

Loneliness exacts a high price. There can be a

sense of desperation and resentment when a spouse alone must care for a sick child or a rebellious child; there can be a sense of desperation and resentment when a spouse alone must face a layoff or middle age without fulfillment. Sexual relationship suffer acutely when spouses are lonely.

Families with one wage are less secure than those in which there are two. A single wage earner is under more pressure to succeed to compete to have to travel to stay at hated job in order to survive unemployment. A second wage earner provides a buffer, so his or her spouse may change jobs or train or retrain. A widowed or divorced spouse without labor force experiences faces a very bleak would financially and psychologically. Who have no further identify to turn to. Finally at any given time we would have many millions more families on welfare if both spouses were not in paid employment. Two wage earners obviously have a much better chance to provide a reasonable standard of living for themselves and their children. Each parent faces a significant chance of widowhood or divorce. Most young men face single parenthood without enough training for the task and without equal rights to custody and child companionship and support.

Less often recognised is the gross deprivation of most men even where there is no widowhood or divorce. Occasionally, we deplore the specter of men governing our nation who have never taken care of a child of an aged parent or a pet or even a plant. Occasionally, if much too rarely, we take note of the fact the that modern managers and modern foremen need to be nurturant sensitive and patient at lest as much as they need to be aggressive brave and though.

We see this perhaps most clearly as we view with concern a generation of women who might become managers without being socialized to take care of other people. It is extremely rare for us to discuss in public what it means for individual men to be cut off from children and other direct, personal, nurturant activities. The belief that men may reasonably spend their lives without the right or expectation of direct caretaking may lead to a variety of damage. One knows many men who do not physically or emotionally take care of themselves, who lose much of their joy in life by being cut off from their feelings, who suffer considerably in childhood, adolescence, and manhood by competing with other males, who have essentially lost the sense of meaning and continuity of life by being cut off from aged parents and children, by being sanitized at every turn from human emotion. The female experiences of separateness and loneliness, bad as they are, seem to me mild compared with the destruction of self involved in out cutting off many men from their nurturant selves and their caring potential.

Work Satisfaction and Leisure Satisfaction. Analyses of work satisfaction indicate that some people value work for the process of working, some for the product, some for the remuneration, some for work-group relations. Some value status, the chance for creativity, the sense of autonomy over one's work. Joy in leisure-time activities is similarly related.

In traditional families each parent has only one work arena in which to seek satisfaction, friends, status, a sense of identity, and a sense of challenge and growth. If the home environment or the paid-work environment happens to provide the right processes, products, remuneration, friends, status, and autonomy for the parents assigned to that environment, all is well. But for many people having only one arena provides a severe sense of constraint. Leisure activities are often similarly constrained. Moreover, the inequity of work-status and leisure-activity status between husband and wife in traditional families means that it is hard for many to maintain the love and comradeship which flourish between equals.

Finally, just the presumption that each individual will conform to the requirements of a stereotyped and arbitrary role is felt by many to be very constricting. This feeling has probably become more pronounced in recent years. In a simple society role differentiation still permitted a wide range of expression. In the specializations of industrialism, much of this range has been lost, so that role requirements have become for many people much more constraining and are felt by many to be destructive to individuals.

Economic and Educational Discrimination Against Women. Of all the difficulties caused by and symbolized by traditional child-care patterns, perhaps the best understood is economic discrimination against women. Discrimination against women is often alleged to occur with respect to education, job recruitment, promotion, benefits, work ambiance, and the wage gap. The index of sex inequality most frequently cited is the wage gap between men and women; women's wages on the average are less than 60% of men's wages. Because the wage gap between men and women is easily quantified, it is the most easily analyzed indicator of sex discrimination. Economists interested in discrimination often begin with some estimate of wage gaps and then seek to explain these gaps by controlling for education, years of experience, entrance into given occupations and promotional patterns, thereafter assigning any residual gap to "pure" or direct discrimination. Many feminists look upon these studies as analyzing indirect discrimination in order to isolate direct discrimination.

How much of gross wage gaps can be attributed directly of indirectly to sex-role differentiation in child care, as distinguished from sex-role differentiation in general? Here again, as with the rest of the discussion above, we cannot be sure exactly what part of discrimination is caused by, and what is symbolized by, differentiation in roles with respect to child care. We do know that, on the average, single women and childfree women have done better with respect to education, labor force participation, promotions, and wages. And we know that these "success" patterns are in general reversed for men. Who typically thrive better when married and with children. But we do not know enough about selection factors or about indirect discrimination. And economists disagree on exactly how to analyze the gross wage gaps. Thus there is no exact one-to-one evidence on the discriminatory importance of sex roles in child care. On the other hand, we do know some of the broad outlines of the effect of child-care patterns and how they may affect economic discrimination.

To begin with, many economists believe that a large part of the wage gap between men and women can be explained by occupational segregation. Women are in general found in certain occupations which pay rather low wages or none at all.

Systematically low wages in "women's" occupations are variously explained by "crowding", "tastes", and human capital theory. "Crowding" is thought to result in lower wages for women because women have unequal access to many jobs. This produces a crowding of women into a few occupations is lower than that of men in other occupations. The "tastes" argument suggests that employers and consumers simply "don't like" women in certain jobs or "assume they are inferior" and therefore discriminate against them. Both of these arguments would suggest that there is psychological reason for denying women access to well-paying positions. Human capital theory suggests that women are on the average paid less than men because they are less productive and that they are less productive primarily because they are less well educated and trained. All of these theories find justification in empirical studies.

In addition to wage gaps produced by occupational segregation, most economists agree that part of the gross wage gap can be explained by differences in real and expected labor force participation-hours per week, weeks per year, years per lifetime. But most now agree that these differences are less important than those rooted in occupational segregation. And most also agree that straightforward unequal pay for equal work is of only minimal importance.

How do our traditional expectations about child care lead to wage gaps? One may raise hypotheses all along the line, with respect to each theory above. Some have suggested that crowding and "discriminatory tastes" arise in part from a desire by males to compensate for not being able to gestate or nurse babies. This theory suggests that men have more need than women to create and control outside the family and that they have a signal dear of competing directly with women because of a primitive fear that they cannot really compete, with respect to creation. With respect to human capital theory, many have suggested that the reason that women ask for and are permitted less education and less valuable training is that they need less education because their chief role is to marry and have children. In the 19th century, prolonged study was widely believed to be too strenuous for female anatomy and also likely to weaken a woman's reproductive capabilities. Although higher education is no longer considered damaging to motherhood, it is still widely considered unnecessary for mothers. Child-care responsibilities and the presumption that women should have full responsibility for children still directly interfere with equal educational opportunities for women.

During the 1970s, in the course of my work in and around universities in New England, I remember many very direct statements on this subject. For example, there was the admissions committee professor at a professional school who would admit women only if they "promise to stay celibate here". Many educational institutions have only recently permitted pregnant women to continue to study. Many others still do not have reasonable provisions for part-time graduate work and residencies for young parents. By the same token, we still find daily stories of women asked in recruitment interviews about their family plans and contraception or stories of women not offered jobs or promotions or raises because of presumptions about their family life.

To the extent that hours per week, weeks per year, and years per lifetime are important in explaining the wage gap, it is easy to see a very direct connection between our traditional child arrangements and labor force participation. With mothers in the paid labor force typically working a much longer total work week than fathers, it is easy to understand the direct conflict between paid and unpaid work.

Another area of economic discrimination where the relationship between labor force participation and traditional child are is very direct has to do with benefits-health care, vacations, pensions, Social Security. Adequate benefits coverage does not yet exist for men, but for women the situation is much worse. Women produce nearly 30% of family incomes; gross national product would rise by another estimated 20% if the unpaid work of women were include in GNP. Yet millions of women are without adequate health care, without vacation time, without appropriate pensions. This happens partly because much part-time work carries no benefits, because unpaid work in the home carries no direct benefits, because women as mothers have been considered their husbands' dependents, and because of the wage gap discussed above, which means that women's benefits, where they exist., are often lower. All these facts follow quite directly from the traditional vision of women as child carers.

Another and similar economic problem concerns our inadequate income tax deductions for child care. Money paid for child care should be reckoned as a business expense, which means it should, be subtracted betore the estimation of taxable income. Instead, and probably partly because child care is traditionally not paid for, we have an inadequate deduction, which constitutes another economic discrimination.

Finally, as we consider economic discrimination,

the subtle importance of traditional child care may be much greater than we know. To the extent that women and men maintain the image of women as dependent child carers, it is easier for us all unconsciously to discriminate against women in paid work.

In addition, the woman whose total work experience has been in unpaid work may herself have a poor idea what she is "worth". As she considers paid work, she may have a tendency to think in terms of her 'next best" occupation, which is to be paid nothing in direct wages. Such women, and men too, may think of her work as "not worth very much", and by extension the work of all women may seem not to be worth very much. When "all women" are imagined to be restricted to "nurturance", it is easier to think of women as all alike; one need not then worry about rewards for individual productivity.

As we consider out own homemaking and child care, which usually have no direct price, some may consider these activities to be "worth" very little, and others may consider them "priceless". Many people in fact argue eloquently that no financial figure can approach the value of human care; they would hate to see all care taking paid for. We find this feeling easily understandable. However, we believe that, if most nurturance is not to be cash paid, it should generally be shared equally between men and women. One can, in other words, believe in the value of child care and all nurturant activities without accepting systematic economic and educational discrimination against women. In fact, it is the premise of this article that one can believe in children and child care, without all of the separateness, loneliness, financial insecurity, deprivation from nurturance, work and leisure dissatisfactions, and discrimination which are at present part of our inheritance from traditional sex roles.

What About Day Care? We have argued that traditional child care may not now be ideal for children and parents and families. Many people, faced with these feelings, advocate universal child care external to the home, available 24 hours per day and subsidized by the government on a sliding fee scale.

Excellent child care would certainly speak to the needs of many children, especially those now left alone, the malnourished, the rat-bitten, the abused. Provision of better care for all children would directly improve the lives of a fourth of our population for a fifth of their lives. It would rescue at least 10% of our children from conditions that we ought to consider intolerable.

With respect to parents, the availability of excellent care would certainly alleviate some of the loneliness and much of the financial insecurity we discussed above. It is an absolute necessity for the 10th of all parents who are single, especially if they work outside the home. However, day-care delivered on a traditional, woman-oriented basis, as it is now, might not so much to alleviate the sense of separateness between men and women, the deprivation from nurturance, the work dissatisfactions, and economic discrimination. In fact, on balance, our present day-care arrangements probably contribute as much to traditional stereotypes as they provide options. In particular, the employment of women in paid as well as unpaid child-care arrangements probably substantiates the occupational segregation which is the strongest source of economic discrimination.

Full-time day-care, on the average about 8.5 hours a day, 42.5 hours per week, probably also causes some feelings of deprivation for some parents. It seems probable that , of they had optimal choices, many parents would prefer to be able to take somewhat more care of their children than is the case with full-time day-care.

We have reviewed paid and unpaid U.S. child-care arrangements, which suggest a strong sex-role differentiation of the work and joy involved in having children. This author believes that this differentiation is one major factor in maintaining all other attributes of sex roles. More options with respect to child care and new socialization patterns for both sexes toward caring for children and others might make a major difference in the quality of life for adults and children. This leads us to a discussion of androgyny.

Androgyny and child care

Androgyny means that low people spend their time should be influenced primarily by skills and interests, not by gender. It would mean that men and women would equally share financial responsibility and child-care and homemaking responsibilities. Equal sharing of responsibilities would not necessarily mean that men and women would exactly divide the laundry and the diapers and the bills. Rather, there would be a social and legal presumption that performance of these duties would be negotiated between spouses, on a continuous lifetime basis, with equal moral rights and responsibilities.

The theoretical basis of androgyny is the proposition that both men and women have both "masculine" and "feminine" potential with regard to character development. There is no presumption that individuals should all be alike, but that everyone has some nurturant and some instrumental potential.

In individual instances, of course, an androgynous society would support responsible childlessness and full-time homemakers that were female, as well as male. But the society as a whole would be set up to support male and female parents as wage-earners and to support male and female wage-earners as parents, in whatever responsible patterns that spouses might choose.

Let us take the example of a young couple with the modal one or two children. In a society which supported young parents to work in half-time or three-quarter-time paid jobs, the family would receive one or one and a half salaries. Suppose both parents worked 30 hours a week in paid jobs. Suppose further that they used child care 10 to 20 hours per week, including evening baby-sitting, and that otherwise they split child-care responsibilities. They would each get to know the children and the skills of homemaking and they would have a chance to spend some time alone together.

With respect to our list of concerns in the section above about the effects of child-care arrangements, androgynous spouses would have a much keener sense of each other's lives. The "learned helplessness" of each sex toward the other's role might generally disappear. Spouses who intimately shared responsibilities might feel much less taken for granted and much less lonely. One can imagine women being very supportive of a spouse's need to relax after the office and men no longer dropping laundry on the floor.

Family financial security would grow, along with family incomes, since lifetime earnings and one's ability to find and keep a job depend much more on continuous years in the labor force than on hours per week. Promotions might come one to three years later for a typical worker who took a three-quarter-time job while the children were small. However, if the typical worker shared family responsibilities with a spouse who also worked three-quarter-time in a paid hob throughout the years of young parenthood, each could expect much higher lifetime earnings than if he or she dropped out for family reponsibilities. Thus the expected later promotions permit much higher family earnings. We would expect that the quality of life for many people would rise, as they gained another arena for friends, status, productivity, and self-image. Both spouses would have one work area at home where there would be considerable autonomy over one's work. Women might gain more sleep; men might gain more options for self-expression and a respite from competition.

Spouse left alone, through death or divorce, would be likely to survive in both paid work and family life. Men who equally cared for their children could have, in practice, more rights with respect to custody and visitation. One can imagine that retirement from child raising and paid work would be much more comfortable under circumstances in which both spouses had a wider range of skills and interests. Mid-life crises might also be less severe, with a wider range of options offered by two sets of skills and two incomes in the family. With respect to discrimination, one may imagine that many of the direct sources of wage and promotional inequality might disappear in an androgynous society. Both men and women would have equal access to education, training, and hobs. Many couples might choose to share family responsibilities so completed that neither spouse ever dropped out of school or a job for family reasons. Other couples might choose to have one or the other spouse as full-time homemaker for a period of time. Nationally, however, we might expect androgynous socialization and work patterns to produce a random distribution of men and women as full-time homemakers. By the same token, sex-based wage differences now attributable to mobility, years of experience, and hours per week in the paid labor force would also disappear as women began to spend their time in similar ways.

The physiological bases for work differentiation seem already much muted. Some jobs requiring great strength might remain forever disproportionately male. These, however, seem unlikely to produce national wage gaps between men and women. If there are hormonal differences of significant importance to work aggressiveness, these may persist. But we will not know to what extent, if at all they are important until we have offered boys and girls equal options in cooperation and assertiveness. One may guess from cross-cultural studies that culture is enormously important and may "wash our" whatever minor hormonal differences exist.

Motivational differences between men and women might be expected to have less and less effect on sex-children and others would find gestation and nursing much less important than lifetime nurturance. Such men might conceivably be some what less driven to create. Women, on the other hand, knowing they would share financial responsibility, might work harder to be recruited, paid, and promoted appropriately.

What would happen to the concentration and perseverance required for extraordinary intellectual, scientific, artistic achievement? One may guess that some people will always choose to stay single and/or childless. Others will find supportive spouses or communes or other families. Many will simply postpone achievement for a year or several years. In any case, the achievements will come to both men and women.

What of total social productivity? Is it true that one must be young to innovate? Would the total number of innovations drop? There is some reason to believe that extraordinary scientific achievements now occur within several years of taking on new intellectual problems; these are not necessarily limited to young people. In modern times, genius often requires extensive teamwork, many building-block experiments, and then a new look. It is not at all clear that having men and women in part-time work for several years would jeopardize creative break throughs over a lifetime; indeed, many very innovative people have waxed and waned in creativitv several times throughout a lifetime.

What probably is very important, from the point of view of social productivity, is that intellectual, artistic, and social genius find option to flower. If we imagine, for example, that scientific, artistic, and caring potentials are randomly distributed among males and females, then we could nearly double the incidence of scientific, artistic, and human achievements by opening all occupations to both sexes. Moreover, while some kinds of achievements seem to require a lifelong, even celibate concentration. Thus children keep some people sane for the laboratory keeps them sane for the children.

Finally, from the point of view of social productivity, we may discover that androgyny provides us with a more caring would. Suppose that more women, socialized to nurturance and cooperation, get into influential jobs? And suppose that we also socialize out young males to expect to care for children and others? Might we see a reordering of values for governance and management?

This article makes no pretense to the notion that sex-role differentiation causes all evil and that androgyny will iron out all pain. If sexism begins to disappear, perhaps we will become caring enough to eliminate racism and other forms of human violence as well, but it seems likely that we will move only slowly at best. Some androgynous couples will divorce , and some men and women will be as miserable with more options as they were with fewer. There may also be children who would flourish more if they saw their parents less. But on balance one may believe that freeing all humans to share in child care on a part-time basis may bring more happiness to children and adults. Children will have a greater chance to be with someone who wants to be with them; both children and adults will be free to explore their caring and inventive selves.

Present-day androgynous couples often find it difficult to combine paid work and family life in an equitable manner. One would therefore recommend changes in social policies which would make it easier for parents to share the responsibilities and advantages of home and paid work.

The first and most basic legal and social change should clearly be the Equal Rights Amendment to the U.S. Constitution. No other single change would be more likely to permit protection of males as nurturant parents as well as protection of women in public life.

With respect to the organization of paid work in our society, many changes are needed. First there should be a reconsideration of what is meant by full time work. At a time of structural as well as cyclical unemployment, it seems reasonable to ask whether full-time work should be redefined as 30 to 35 hours per week. This alone would permit young parents more time to share child care as well as spreading the work of the nation among more different people.

Part-time work, part-week, or part-year needs systematic support for both sexes. Discrimination against part-time workers, in terms of promotion and benefits should be forbidden. Benefits should be prorated including pensions. In general we should take those steps that support "bumpy" career ladders so that parents work longer and shorter work weeks depending on the stage in their life cycles. Mandated seniority and promotional patterns in union contracts and tenure ladders for instances should take account to periods of part time work. At least 10% of government jobs should be set aside for part time workers.

Employers have not traditionally been enthusiastic about the extra expense of extra sets of paper work involved in hiring proportionately more workers. However, we believe we need extensive research to see whether productivity per hour may not be higher for part time workers. it may be that in many jobs part time workers repay the extra expense involved in having proportionately more people.

We need many more flexible time jobs. Some employers can adopt the system whereby all employees may choose to come in between 7 a.m and 10 a.m and to leave between 3 p.m and 6 p.m. Others may wish to designate only certain jobs for flexible times of a standard type of or for individually designed times.

Some jobs can be designed for people who need flexible, short term leaves of absence. For instance we need more under time jobs whereby employees can agree to accept 2% 4% or 6% less salary on a prorated basis in return for 5, 10 or 15 days leave of absence on a planned approved and voluntary basis.

One important structure to support part-time and flexible hour jobs is a well run posting system within organizations. A posting system means that all job openings are widely advertised for a certain period of time within a given organization. Supervisors describe the job opening including a description of whether a job can be part time shared appointment, flexible hours, or under time job. Such posting systems also serve the purpose of supporting career development and perhaps should be low or fostered by tax incentives.

In times of economic prosperity employers have been reluctant to institute work structures supportive of family life. However, with high turnover, worker discontent and budget crunches many employers are considering shortened work weeks and flexible hiring plans as ways to raise productivity and cut costs. Under time and part year jobs in particular offer a chance to plan leaves of absence during work lulls; well-run posting systems help to alleviate the pain of retrenchment while helping to protect long term employees.

Parental leave needs further change in most American firms. We should consider the parental insurance systems of Sweden, whereby parents have a right to paid leave up to seven months after a birth. We should further consider the Swedish system of parental sick leave for children's illnesses. At a minimum maternity leave should be treated as a temporary disability. This minimum improvement should also include unpaid leave for either parent up to six months postpartum, and the right to use some days of personal sick leave for children illnesses, for children under 12.

Further changes should include reform of child labour and insurance laws so that children can work in nonexploitative apprenticeships. Our present segregation of children under age 16 from many workplaces has the effect of keeping are groups unnecessarily apart. We also need changes is Social Security so that people over 65 can legally continue to work and earn, so that more grandparents are availabl to mote children.

The definition of work itself needs change. It unpaid homemaking and chair care by full-time homemakers were reckoned into the GNP and defined as work we might pave the way for redefinitions of Social Security welfare pensions and other benefits. If Social Security were vested individually in all responsible workers, it would be easier for both men and women to consider full time homemaking without all the present risk to displaced (abandoned, divorced and widowed) homemakers. If child rearing were seen as socially constructive work. Aid to Families of

Dependent Children would become payment for child care, with attendant benefits and pensions, akin to military service, military benefits, and military retirement. Moreover if full-time homemakers were seen as responsible workers, socially as worthwhile as military employees, we would have a stronger theoretical reason for a universal health plan for all Americans.

Changes in the tax laws could also help family programs. Further tax write-offs for employers for family support structures are badly needed. Work-and training-related child-care expenses should also be allowed where payments are made to relatives. Work- and training-related child-care allowances should be automatic for families earning incomes below the poverty level, continuing on a reduced basis to a level up to 1.5 times the poverty level.

Finally, we plainly need changes in marriage and divorce laws. In further support of displaced homemakers of either sex, we should consider government support for retraining parents who have been full-time at home for say, 10 or more years. And all the myriad laws surrounding custody, alimony, visitation and child support should be changed toward equity between men and women.

How could we support further attitudinal change toward androgyny? First, we need much more national information and debate. Many ardent feminists of both sexes understand women in engineering without understanding men in nursing and child care. Yet it is obvious that women will never be equal in formerly male occupations without a mirror image change occurring for men. If this were not to occur-if men were not to have equal opportunity in formerly female occupations—women would wind up doing three-fourths of the nations work. This fact and its attendant implications for socialisation patterns and educational curricula need the widest possible discussion.

Fortunately, we may presume that androgyny itself may foster adrogyny. Early generations of children raised by both men and women, who see caring men and self-reliant women, have androgynous role models to emulate. Today's parents. Knowing that a daughter has one chance in two of becoming a chief wage-earner for at least part of her life, are beginning to support daughters in androgynous patters. This in turn has inevitable consequences for the lives of men. Perhaps if we succeed in social policies that support androgyny, we will reap the benefits in terms of increased options for men and women and children. If we lag in supporting androgyny we may see yet more anguish, in terms of personal bewilderment and of children left more and more alone.

10

Committee on Child Care

The Central Social Welfare Board, at the instance of the Union Ministry of Education, decided at its 30th Meeting held in October 1960, to appoint a Committee to prepare a comprehensive plan for the care and training of children in the age group 0-6. The report of the Committee contains the following chapters:

1. Family and the Nation.
2. Child Population and Family Planning.
3. The Background and Concept of Child Care and Neglect.
4. Infant Mortality and Diseases Amongst Children.
5. Health and Infant Welfare.
6. The Pre-school.
7. Handicapped Children.
8. Personnel and Training Programmes.
9. Organisation and Management of Child Welfare Programmes and Institutions.
10. Children's Recreations: Art, literature and Play.
11. Recommendations.

Terms of Reference of the Committee on Child Care for the Age Group-Birth to 6 Plus

1. To study in the light of changing socio-economic conditions in the country care and upbringing of children in the family and the community with particular references in the home and in the neighbourhood.

2. To examine the problems of children in need of special care and protection and to recommend measures for providing comprehensive child care services for them.

3. To evaluate the nature, extent and distribution of existing child welfare services with special reference to the management, corporate non-official and pattern of pre-schools.

4. (1) To study and evaluate the standards of pre-school education with reference to:

   (1) The pattern of staffing; (ii) The curricula and methods of teaching adopted; (iii) the type of equipment available and the manner and extent of its use; and (iv) Programme of recreation, rest, nutrition, health care and instruction.

   (II) to work out a tentative plan for the development of pre-school education for the next five or ten years with estimates of cost.

5. To study the existing facilities for training of child welfare workers in terms of the number of centres required and contents and standards of training and to suggest a long term training programme for child welfare workers on an uniform basis.

6. To work out a plan for the manufacture of a

standard recreational and educational equipment at moderate cost, suited to the requirements of Indian children. This could be linked up with the socio-economic programme of the Central Social Welfare Board.

7. To assess the financial position of child welfare institutions for this age group to study their pattern of income and expenditure and to assess the problems of grant-in-aid, the nature and volume of assistance required and the period for which it would be necessary.

8. To recommend a pattern for the reorganization and extension of the programme of community and institutional services for the proper physical, mental and emotional development of the child in the first six years, keeping in view the continuity of services for children that will follow from 6 to 11 and 12 years to adulthood.

9. To suggest methods of co-ordinate among the large number of agencies working in the field of child welfare.

Recommendations for pre-schools

1. That pre-school education must be single-mindedly devoted to the true welfare, growth and development of the human child as a vital organism, and a unit of the human species.

2. That the concepts of pre-school philosophy and principles are appropriate tom Indian conditions and needs that children must be healthy an active within heir family and community environments and grow up and develop during childhood to receive education and become worthy citizens of the nation.

3. That the system of training must correspond to the fundamental needs of the child's comprehensive growth and development irrespective of any social, economic, political or philosophical considerations.
4. That the pre-school programme should be based upon five factors which have been universally accepted and which are stated below:
   (i) Heredity and environment of the child must receive very great attention because the growth and development of the child is largely dependent on these two factors.

   (ii) That child at all times must live in an atmosphere which is full of joy, contributing to its total happiness.

   (ii) The child must grow up and develop in condition of freedom.

   (iv) The child needs activity in order to spend its energy and to expand its total capacity and abilities, thus accumulating experiences which contribute to its total growth and development.

   (v) The child needs protection and assistance of parents and other competent persons who are aware of the special needs of children during the pre-school age.
5. In order to increase the number of pre-schools in the whole of India including urban, rural and sylvan areas, it is necessary to organizationally promote self-sufficient pre-schools which could be organized, if possible without the assistance of the State to be managed by regional communities in urban neighbourhoods and large villages. A

national pre-schools association be created for this purpose.

6. Pre-schools shall be started in urban areas, where people can pay the cost of education of the children.

7. Responsibility for starting pre-schools should be left to voluntary organizations with adequate assistance from the Government.

8. (i) That pre-schools should be of the following types:

   (a) A half day organization to be developed "The Minimum Standard Pre-school". A pre-school of minimum standard should provide a playground look after the health and cleanliness of children, inculcate in good habits and correct behaviors, and provide such opportunities for training like nature study and other subjects which can be easily dealt with by reasonably trained teachers and Balsevikas.

   (b) Standard pre-schools following some kind of systems like the Montessori, the pre-basic, Azzisi and any other system suitable to rural areas, and any type of pre-school using programmes, methods and techniques suitable for different type of environments in urban areas.

   (The true meaning of pre-basic should imply the acceptance of the principle of activity initiated and develop by a number of psychologists and educationsists of Vienna. The types of activities must be suitable to the needs of the child and the community.)

(c) A pre-school project attached to the village primary school, to be located as far as possible in a separate structure so that classes of the pre-school and primary school are not held together.

(d) Infant classes in primary schools and high schools, with training and programme modified to conform to principles and programmes of the pre-school.

(e) Open-air pre-schools with playgrounds may be created where facilities and resources are inadequate, or where there are inadequate numbers of children to promote a pre-school as a unit.

(f) Pre-schools attached to institutions where unattached women with children are provided with boarding and lodging facilities.

(ii) Special pre-schools in urban areas for sub-normal, feeble-minded and problem children with behaviour disorders.

(iii) Special types of pre-schools to help in the training and rehabilitation of handicapped children.

(iv) Pre-schools attached to prisons for women with their children.

(v) Pre-school with a high standard of service for areas where communities of ex-criminal group live.

(vi) Pre-schools promoted as a special treatment for areas where juvenile delinquency is extensively present.

(vii) Pre-schools organized in large housing schemes where a number of rooms and tenements are available for their use. Where there is no space for playgrounds, terraces may be suitably adjusted for the purpose in order to provide safety for the children.

(9) That all under-privileged children should be given an opportunity for pre-school education but it is not desirable to create separate pre-schools for them.

(10) That a common nomenclature for all pre-school s in not desirable; but when names are give to pre-schools they should not as far as possible, be associated with names of systems and types of equipment used in each pre-school.

(11) It is not desirable for pre-schools to have a very large number of children and as far as possible a pre-school should not have more than four units.

(12) That during the whole period of stay of a child in a pre-school it may go through three or four stages of training. Each state of the child's training in a pre-school must conform to his physical conditions and nature of growth and development.

(13) That pre-school should as far as possible be located near places where a large number of families reside, and as far as possible, they may belong to regional communicates, and may be entrusted to their care for management and supervision.

(14) That where children have to walk to the pre-school they should not be expected to go more

than one mile from their place of residence each day.

(15) Transport facilities may be provided by institutions which are self-sufficient in their resources.

(16) That the presence of natural surroundings in necessary for the physical growth and emotional development of children, and when pre-school are not open air schools, gardens and playgrounds should be attached to them.

(17) Pre-school in rural areas should be located in village with a minimum population of about 500 persons. Preference should be given to village which agree to give a site for the structure and playground and bear part cost of structure of at least provide labour for construction.

In tribal areas where people live in hamlets which are located at considerable distances with small population, the pre-schools should be located in villages where hamlets are close together, and where it will be possible for the children to walk small distances to attend the pre-school.

(18) That heavy capital expenditure should not be incurred for the construction of pre-schools. Even open air schools, low cost structures or gardens or open spaces be considered adequate for the use of children.

(19) That whenever possible simple structures may be constructed and they could be 'kutcha' structures in rural areas, using local material for their construction. The plan of the pre-school should

allow sufficient space for kitchen and a washing place, dining and siesta.

(20) That a pre-school must have a playground, at least two rooms, a tap, bathroom, lavatory and urinals.

(21) That municipalities, landlords, owners of public places like temples, churches and all citizens must do everything in their power to see that space and shelter are not denied to children for play and pre-schools.

(22) ' at for pre-schools with more available space about 100sq ft of ground and garden per child are needed for open air activities. For indoor activities there should be an assembly hall, which can also be used for siesta purposes, as well as space for group activities and indoor meetings. A store room and a kitchen, an office room, a staff room, and an isolation room could always be useful. There should be a locker room for children, if possible, adequate washing and bathing accommodation, and taps and toilet for all children, should be provided. At least one lavatory is needed for every 12 to 15 children.

(23) That routine programme of activities of the pre-school must always be adopted to suit the place, the climate, the ability of teacher and the wish, of children, and pre-schools are invariably good weather institutions, and children should not be called to participate in activities of pre-school during inclement weather when there are heavy rains or cold. Pre-schools should function during seasons and months suitable for different types or pre-school activities.

(24) That pre-schools should start their day in the morning assembly so that all children may gather, meet each other, and enjoy companionship. Daily programmes should be planned in advance by the pre-school teachers and varieties of subjects and activities should be introduced everyday like play activities, learning activities, handwork activities, practical, school service etc. Children must enjoy open air and outdoor life as much as they can. The time allotted to different types of activities should vary according to the capacities of children to give attention and their interest in activities or subject which are handled by the teacher.

(25) That children must participate in all important activities of the whole community, and this must be an important part of all pre-school activities.

(26) That at least a midday meal or snack should be served at pre-school, and three meals should be given, if the family and the community are willing to contribute towards the expenses of a light morning breakfast with milk lunch, and light evening snack with fruits.

(27) That a carefully study must be made of the sleeping habits of children at home; and there must be a daily siesta of 90 to 120 minutes after the midday meal. When the pre-school works only for half a day, and when parents insist that children should return home for their afternoon lunch, then parental education must make them realize that the child must have sleep and rest at home during the afternoon.

(28) That to meet all pre-school expenses, local

contributions should be obtained from the community in cash, kind, labour or service towards Programme of construction, nutrition, instruction, excursion and camps.

(29) There should be a team of the following scientists to assist pre-school workers training Programme and counsellors of pre-schools. Psychologists, Pediatricians, Nutrition experts, Educationists, Sociologist, Biologist, and other scientists dealing with the methodology of pre-school training. Their services may be requisitioned from regional universities.

(30) That Balsevikas should be young women, preferably under 25 years of age at the time of employment, as small child normally responds affectionately to young persons or very old persons. The employment of young men should not be ruled out for pre-school work, because they are useful as instructors for hand-work, playground activities and pre-school social service.

(31) That pre-school with two or three units and not exceeding four units should have a Mukhys Shikshika, or Headmistress or Principal.

(32) A larger number of pre-schools and institutions with a high standard of child care and training programme will require a Director for the pre-school whole in rural areas persons will be required to director, organize, and supervise a large number of pre-schools in each district. A woman district welfare officer should be entrusted with this work.

(33) That term like 'ayah' or, servants are inappropriate

for pre-schools, but assistance and helpers or 'Sahayika' are required for the maintenance of cleanliness, helping children to bathe and wash themselves, for the preparation of service of meals, cleaning of utensils, and helping to look after unmanageable children.

(34) Pre-school attended by children with behaviour problems require a special person on the staff trained in psychology.

National Policy for Children

The Statement of National Policy for children is intended to serve as a 'pole star' to guide the official and non-official agencies alike in regard to the direction in which they should move for achieving full and integrated development of our children who constitute our most valuable asset for posterity. National policy has been enunciated in Government Resolution No. FL - 14/74-CDD, dated August 22, 1974 which was tabled in both the Houses of Parliament on August 26, 1974. The Resolution was communicated to State Governments/ Administration of Union Territories. Resolution No. 1- 14/74-CDD. The Government of India have had under consideration the question of evolving a national policy for the welfare of children. After due consideration, it has decided to adopt the policy enunciated below.

The nation's children are a supremely important asset. Their nature and solicitude are our responsibility. Children's programme should find a prominent part on our national plans for the development of human resources, so that our children grow up to become robust citizens, physically fit, mentally alert and morally healthy, endowed with the skills and motivations needed by society. Equal opportunities for development to all children during the period of growth should be our aim, for this would serve our larger purpose or reducing inequality and ensuring social justice.

Goals: The needs of children' and our duties towards them have been expressed in the Constituted. The Resolution on a National Policy of Education, which has been adopted by Parliament, gives direction to State Policy on the educational needs of children. We are also party to the U.N. Declaration of the Rights of the Child. The goals set out in these documents can reasonably be achieved by judicious and efficient use of the available national resources. Keeping in view these goals, the Government of India adopts this resolution on the National Policy for Children.

Policy and measures: It shall be the policy of the State to provide adequate services to children, both before and after birth and through the period of growth, to ensure their full physical, mental and social development. The State shall progressively increase the scope of such services so that within a reasonable time, all children in the country enjoy optimum condition for their balanced growth. In particular, the following measures shall be adopted towards the attachment of these objectives:

(i) All children shall be covered by a comprehensive health programme.

(ii) Programmes shall be implemented to provide nutrition services with the object of removing deficiencies in the diet of children.

(iii) Programmes will be undertaken for the general improvement of the health and for the care, nutrition and nutrition education of expectant and nursing mothers.

(iv) The State shall take steps to provide free and compulsory education for all children upto the age of 14 for which a time-bound programme will be drawn up consistent with the availability of resources. Special efforts will be made to reduce the prevailing wastage and stagnation in schools, particularly in the case of girls and children of the weaker sections of society. The programme of informal education for pre-school children from such sections will also be taken up.

(v) Children who are not able to take full advantage of formal schools education shall be provided other forms of education suited to their requirements.

(vi) Physical education, games, sports and other types of recreational as well as cultural and scientific activities shall be promoted in schools, community centres and such other institutions.

(vii) To ensure equality of opportunity, special assistance shall be provided to all children belonging to the weaker sections of the society, such as children belonging to the scheduled castes and scheduled tribes and those belonging to the economically weaker sections, both in urban and rural areas.

(viii) Children who are socially handicapped, who have become delinquent or have been forced to take to begging or are otherwise in distress, shall be provided facilities for education, training and rehabilitation and will be helped to become useful citizen.

(ix) Children shall be protected against neglect, cruelty and exploitation.

(x) No child under 14 years shall be permitted to be engaged in any hazardous occupation or be made to undertake heavy work.

(xi) Facilities shall be provided for special treatment, education, rehabilitation and care of children who are physically handicapped, emotionally distributed or mentally retarded.

(xii) Children shall be given priority for protection and relief in times of distress of natural calamity.

(xiii) Special programmes shall be formulated to spot, encourage and assist gifted children, particularly those belonging to the weaker sections of society.

(xiv) Existing laws should be amended so that in all legal disputes, whether between parents or institutions, the interests of children are given paramount consideration.

(xv) In organising services for children, efforts would be directed to strengthen family ties so that fully potentialities of growth of children are realised within the normal family, neighborhood and community environment.

Priority in programme formation. In formulating programmes in different sectors, priority shall be give to programmes relating to

(a) Preventive and promotive aspects of child health.

(b) Nutrition for infants and children in the pre-school age along with nutrition for nursing and expectant mothers.

(c) Maintenance, education and training of orphan and destitute children.

(d) Creches and other facilities for the care of children working or ailing mothers; and

(e) Core, education, training and rehabilitation of handicapped children.

Constitution of national children's board. During the last two decades we have made significant progress in the provision of services for children on the lines detailed above. There has been considerable expansion in the health, nutrition, education and welfare services. Rise in the standard of living, wherever it occurred, has indirectly met children's basic needs to some extent. But all this work needs a focus and a forum for planning and review, and proper coordination of the multiplicity of services striving to meet the needs of children. A national Children's Board shall be constituted to provide this focus and to ensure at different levels continuous planning, review and coordination of all the essential services. Similar Boards may also be constituted at the State level.

Role of voluntary organizations. The Government shall endeavour that adequate resources are provided for child welfare programmes and appropriate schemes are undertaken. At these same time, voluntary organizations engaged in the field of child welfare will continue to have the opportunity to develop, either on their own or with State assistance, the field of education, health recreation and social welfare endeavour of the State to encourage to strengthen voluntary action so that State and voluntary efforts complement each other. The resources of voluntary organisations trusts, charities and religious and other endowments would have to be tapped to the extent possible for promoting and developing child welfare programmes.

Legislative and administrative action. To achieve the above aims, that State will provide necessary legislative and administrative support. Facilities for research and training of personnel will be developed to meet the needs of the expanding programmes and to improve the effectiveness of the service.

People's participation. The Government of India trusts that the policy enunciated in this statement will receive the support and cooperation of all sections the people and of organisations working for children. The Government of India also calls upon the citizens, state governments, local bodies, educational institutions and voluntary, organisations to play their part in the overall effort to attain these objectives.

Index